YOU CAN WORK IT OUT!

Skills and Wisdom for
Conflict Resolution in Relationships

Robert Kallus, LMFT

Hope, Courage, Strength

Dedication

The book is dedicated to the memory of my parents, Ignatz and Rose Kallus, survivors of Nazi concentration camps, who, like many millions of others, knew something about conflict.

Acknowledgements

This book would not exist without the encouragement and inspiration of my many friends and colleagues. Among them are Frank Lott; Dr. Monte and Beth Cox and their children, Rachel, Joel and Sarah; Lew Moore, PhD and the faculty and staff of the Harding University Marriage and Family Therapy Department in Searcy, Arkansas; Rob Salley, PhD; Ray Crowder; Marvin Maupin; Matthew and Janine French; Lorna Hecker, PhD; Col. (ret.) Kathy Platoni, PsyD; and my editor and consultant, Jessie Lucier.

Special thanks go to my wonderful student interns, Emily Friedman, Ian Norris and Ashlyn Houser, who provided invaluable assistance in graphic design, technology and stylistics.

To all these special people and others too numerous to mention, I extend appreciation and gratitude.

Preface

"Do not conform any longer to the pattern of this world.
Instead, be transformed by the renewing of your mind." - Romans 12: 2

"A problem cannot be solved from the same level of consciousness that created it.
We must learn to see the world anew." - Albert Einstein

Does conflict bother you, worry you or frighten you? Do you and your spouse, partner or child go round and round and never get anywhere? Have you had enough of that?

Conflicts continue to afflict us on every level of life. You probably know the saying, "It's a jungle out there." The very idea of a jungle connotes danger. Sometimes relationships can feel dark and threatening, and it seems the light of hope has disappeared forever. Wouldn't it be wonderful if the jungle could be transformed into a sunlit garden?

If the answer is yes, here's a fact you should know. Avoiding conflict, which most of us are conditioned to do, is not always the answer. Habitual avoidance of conflict can lead to relationship failure. While certain conflicts should be avoided, others require attention. The trick is to distinguish one from the other.

This work is meant to help you feel confident and strong, so you will never again avoid facing conflicts … that is, in the cases when a conflict should be addressed.

Part of the problem is that most people do not intuitively handle conflict well, and few of us are shown a healthy example by our parents. If we are wise, we can choose to learn the skills that get us to talk, listen and stay cool when conflict erupts. Often, that requires a change in attitude and behavior.

While it is normal for change to feel uncomfortable, please hang in there. Actually, you probably know how to do that. You probably didn't give up the bicycle the first time you fell off. Applying the skills and insights contained here will help you make the changes more easily than you may have expected.

As you change just one behavior or attitude, you will build on that change. With every success you will be more and more comfortable addressing conflicts directly, rather than avoiding them.

In Part 2, all the anecdotes are based on actual cases, and all the names are made up, as you'll soon notice. Some chapters offer conflict resolution tips while others do not. There is a reason for that. If you are motivated enough, you will go looking for answers yourselves. And when you uncover the answers - they are not hard to find - the changes you make are more likely to stick with you.

Check out books, audios, videos and the internet. In this day and age, anyone who can read can search out solutions in addition to what is provided here.

The Foundation of This Work

"The words of the reckless pierce like swords,
but the tongue of the wise brings healing." - Proverbs 12: 18

The ideas and methods contained here rest on evidence-based practice as well as proven theories, such as the theory that the brain can adapt and be 'rewired' at virtually any point in one's life. This capacity, called neuroplasticity, is a fact. Thus, there is hope for people who doubt that they can change. Further, we know that behavior, mind, body and emotions are all interconnected. This is the mind-body connection. A change in one part prompts the others to change.

But this book is not just based on science. The Greek philosopher, Plato, defines wisdom as "the conjunction of knowledge and virtue." We can learn much from him and others. But, as a believer in the God of the Bible, it is biblical principles, rather than secular teachings, which influenced this work. Additional influences include contained in other world religions. Some of them teach us to honor the divine nature within each person. Native American cultures emphasize respect for the natural world given to us by the Great Spirit. Others emphasize mindfulness, compassion, letting go, acceptance and gratitude.

Interestingly, modern science supports such notions. For example, a University of California study reports that people who carry an 'attitude of gratitude' enjoy a quality of life superior to people who do not. This principle appeared in New Testament Scripture nearly two thousand years ago (See Philippians, ch. 4:8). The ancient practice of transcendental meditation was proved beneficial in numerous ways by Dr. Herbert Benson of Harvard University's College of Medicine. The same is true of mindfulness meditation, which is recommended by many physicians for help with healing.

Having worked with countless couples of varied races, ethnicities and religions, one thing has stood out: couples who share a common faith usually resolve conflict faster and better than people who do not. Couples whose relationship lacks a legitimate moral foundation are much more likely to fail.

As you learn to handle conflict effectively, consider the possibility that a divine dimension really does exist, and that you can have access to its infinite power by means of prayer, meditation, study and doing good to others. You may find that prayer and meditation - possibly the most effective of all stress management strategies - will open doors to wisdom and peace.

Let's get started.

TABLE OF CONTENTS

Start with a Positive Statement or Question - P. 40
Before trying to resolve a conflict, set a positive tone. This section tells you how.

Name the Conflict - P. 41
Poor communication is a problem. But it's usually the tip of the iceberg.

Check Yourself First - P. 42
Your mind-body state directly affects your ability to handle conflict. Do not try to defuse an explosive situation when you feel tense.

Do Not Assume - P. 43
When we assume we know the other person's feelings or motives, we are usually wrong.

Your Inner Language - Pp. 44-45
Become aware of your self-defeating beliefs, expectations and thought patterns.

"I Know What You Want" - P. 46
Claiming to 'know' the other person's motives provokes a defensive response.

Projection - P. 47
Do you assume that your child, spouse or partner is like you? How often are you right?

Lend a Hand - P. 48
Personal change is impossible without positive feedback. Help your spouse, child or partner by encouraging small changes.

A Tip for Blended Families - P. 49
If you're in a blended family, this illustration from my case files may interest you.

Respect - P. 50
Respect is not just one thing.

Assertive vs. Aggressive - P. 51
When you assert your needs without being aggressive, you'll see great results.

Power and Status - P. 52
Domination hampers conflict resolution.

Stay Focused - P. 53
Going off on tangents is a common error. One issue at a time, please.

Defeating the Bully - P. 89
Defeating the bully is not always about fighting back. The power of the mind can do the trick.

Dependency - P. 90
 If you are more emotionally dependent than the other person, you have less power.

When Sharing Yourself, Be Wise - P. 91
Be direct in addressing a relationship conflict; and be selective about the people you confide in.

PART 3 - More Stuff

PART 1

A Two-Part Approach to Resolving Conflict

The Short-Term Approach: Coping with Conflict

If you attended public school in the United States, you took part in monthly fire drills. At the sound of the bell or buzzer, you and your fellow students knew what to do. And the staff followed the directions of the emergency manager. Everyone was trained by this regular procedure to act in an orderly way.

You may also remember that fire extinguishers were placed on the walls throughout the school — in the cafeteria, the kitchen, the hallways, the science lab, etc.

What if your school never practiced fire drills, and one fine day, you smelled smoke and heard the buzzer? Chaos might ensue: running, shoving, general confusion and even injuries.

The monthly fire drill - which is actually a kind of conflict management strategy - prepared us to react correctly, thus reducing the likelihood of turmoil.

Additionally, in the event of a fire, we also need to know how to put it out. Hence, the fire extinguisher. That is how we cope with the emergency as it's happening.

We need to draw from both approaches. Through managing - the continuous training of good habits, right thinking and lifestyle choices - we are able to respond to conflict with increased ease. Coping - drawing from skills and knowledge to de-escalate - helps us settle a conflict as it's taking place.

The Short-Term Approach consists of five proven-effective communication and conflict resolution skills. As you use them, remember the following key principles.

1. In moments that matter, you must slow down the communication process. As you speak, take time to notice the other person's reactions. More importantly, after the other person has spoken, take time before you respond.

2. Do not provoke a negative reaction from the other person. Such reactions include defensiveness, shutting down and lashing out with criticism or disrespect. The Rules of Engagement Questionnaire in Part 3 will help you identify your provocative behaviors.

3. Emotional self-regulation is essential. Do not attempt to handle a conflict or talk about an important matter when you are upset. At such times, the following skills are not usable. The Long-Term Approach describes how to restore relaxation and balance.

Reading this section, imagine a fictional couple, Sam and Julie, who can't seem to stop arguing.

The Five-Second Rule

When Sam or Julie senses that an argument is about to erupt, one or both of them will say or signal to the other to use the 5 second rule, which goes like this:

Sam talks, Julie listens. Julie gives Sam her full attention. No multitasking, no interrupting. She does not react in any way - no eye rolls, no sighs and no gestures, except to nod and let him know she's listening. If Julie hears something she wants to reply to, and she thinks she'll forget, she jots down a quick note. If Sam says something that is false or upsetting, she takes a deep breath to calm herself and keeps listening. When Sam is done talking, Julie waits up to five seconds. In that time, she takes a deep breath before responding.

Next, Julie speaks. Sam listens calmly, just as Julie did. And that's how it goes until they believe they have cooled off and can start talking casually again.

When practiced with patience, this exercise will rid you of bad habits, such as over-reacting, preparing your answer and interrupting.

The Reflecting Statement

Now, after using the 5-Second Rule, what is the best way to respond?

During an argument, clear communication is vital. To promote a respectful conversation, Sam and Julie will be wise to communicate two important things to each other:

First, "I heard you."
Second, "I want to understand you."

In order to do that, they will reflect, or 'mirror' what the other person said. When Julie is finished talking, Sam might say something like:

"I want to be sure I'm understanding you. It sounds like you're saying,
_____, Did I get that right?"

Sam might repeat her words exactly, or paraphrase them. The purpose is to assure her that he cares enough to hear her out, and that he wants to understand her - without judging, criticizing, or defending himself. This is powerful. Add it to the 5-second rule, and notice the benefits.

Stop ◆ Breathe ◆ Re-Think

This third tool is another way of helping Sam and Julie respond calmly and thoughtfully when either of them feels triggered.

First and foremost, they must learn to stop the instant defensive response. This is accomplished by first sensing that they've been triggered. Usually, this involves a physical sensation: a knot in the stomach, a tense jaw, clenched fist, tightness in the chest or burning ears. Such sensations cue them to do something to interrupt the stress response, and move into the relaxation response. Sam might wear a rubber band around his wrist, which he snaps the moment he senses that he's been triggered. Or he might prefer to visualize a large STOP sign. Or smack himself on the forehead - not too hard.

That's the STOP part of it. You know yourself. What physical STOP signal would work for you?

Second, the person who's been triggered takes a deep breath. Breathing deeply cuts short the stress response and activates the relaxation response. This is the BREATHING part of it.

Thirdly, re-think what just happened. After stopping the reaction and taking a deep breath, we can think clearly. And only when we're thinking clearly can we positively re-think spin what the other person said or did.

Here are some examples of thoughts that will help to re-think a negative reaction.

> Am I jumping to a conclusion?
> Am I assuming?
> Did she really mean that the way I think she did?
> Is this a battle I need to fight?
> Maybe I should ask for clarification.
> Did I do or say something to trigger her?
> Maybe he's upset with something I don't know about.
> How can I help her?

Do not judge or second-guess yourself with questions like, "Am I being petty or selfish?" Simply redefine what just happened after you've moved into the relaxation response. The more you do this, the more you'll appreciate it.

The Limited Time-Out

Arguments can escalate to a boiling point in seconds. Whenever you notice that emotions have taken over, stop talking and tell the other person you need a break. Tell him/her how much time you need, and that you're going to be ready to talk again after you've cooled off. Literally, tell the other person something like, "I need a half-hour. I'm going for a walk (or whatever you need to do) and I will be back and ready to talk again at _____ o'clock."

Communicating how much time you need in order to cool down reassures the other person that you're not giving up. Rather, you are demonstrating self-control. This is a powerful positive message. On the contrary, when you exhibit a lack of self-control, you damage trust.

The "I" Statement

Trust is the foundation of any close relationship, and mishandling conflict breaks trust. Fortunately, trust can be regained. (See **Building Bridges of Trust** in Part 3). One sure way to regain trust is to show the other person you mean them no harm. Never point out the other person's bad behavior. Allow yourself to be vulnerable and let the other person see and hear your vulnerability. Take off your emotional armor, let down your guard and be honest about what you feel. This can be risky, if the other person is in an agitated emotional state. Wait until you are both calm and relaxed, and then use the skill you're about to learn.

The "I" Statement helps to express upsets without provoking defensiveness. This approach works. It's simply a statement about what you're feeling emotionally. No judging, attacking, accusing, blaming or threatening.

At first this may feel unnatural. Don't let that put you off. Throughout your life you've had to take on things that didn't feel natural. Much like learning to talk, walk and ride a bike, if you use this skill faithfully and correctly, you'll see the benefits soon enough.

Stating your feelings honestly invites the other person to respond with his or her feelings. In addition, the other person will have to say whether he or she cares how you feel. This skill helps prepare the way for harmonious problem-solving.

When to use The "I" Statement:

When logic and reason - not your emotions - are in control. It's most effectively used at an appropriate time and place.

Why to use it:

The "I" statement is a brief and simple way to express what you feel emotionally. When used correctly, it will not provoke defensiveness.

DO NOT USE THIS SKILL:

> **To de-escalate a heated conflict.**
> **To judge or evaluate others, or to express an opinion or belief.**
> **To describe or define what the other person wants or cares about.**

After expressing the emotion by saying "I felt" or "I feel", <u>DO NOT ADD</u> "like" or "that".

Incorrect: "I feel like you're trying to hide something from me."
Correct: "When you don't share our financial papers with me, I feel anxious."

Incorrect: "I feel that your behavior at Thanksgiving dinner was atrocious."
Correct: "When you raised your voice during Thanksgiving dinner, I felt embarrassed."

Hint 1: If you can substitute the words, "I think" in place of "I feel that" or "I feel like," and the sentence still makes sense, you're doing it incorrectly.

Hint 2: If the other person reacts defensively, it's possible that you didn't really express an emotion, unless the other person is just plain mean-spirited. Those people do exist.

Why does the "I" statement work? Remember Sam and Julie? Imagine that they're arguing and Sam uses the "I" Statement to say what he's feeling. Julie has two options. Either she cares how he feels or she does not. The beauty of this way of communicating is that it creates a softer landing, so to speak, for the message you're trying to send. It's neither harsh nor threatening. Done correctly, it will not provoke defensiveness.

As you use these skills, you'll see that people will respond more positively than you expected. This will reinforce your motivation to turn the skills into healthy habits.

IMPORTANT NOTE: This skill is available only when you are in a calm and balanced mind-body state. The following section will tell you how to achieve that state. Before reading further, you may want to look at the detailed explanation of the "I" statement in *The "I" Statement Reloaded* in Part 3.

The Long-Term Approach: Managing Conflict

Remember the example of the fire drill? That effective habit was imposed on you for your safety. The Long-Term Approach is meant to help you create your own good habits that will make it easier to cope when conflict arises.

In general, do you feel easy-going or tense? This question is key because your handling of conflict depends on your state of being - mentally, emotionally and physically. Irritability, tension, pain, apathy and sadness cloud the mind. But a calm and positive mind-body state helps you think clearly.

You have the ability and the right to take your well-being into your own hands. Make a promise to yourself to adopt daily habits which will produce a healthy mind-body state.

A daily practice of the following habits will help you achieve and maintain a state of well-being and a healthy lifestyle.

Behavioral	Mental / Emotional	Social
Regular physical exercise	Music and art	Spiritual fellowship
Healthy diet	Reading	Family meals
Good sleep habits	Hearing inspirational talks	Volunteering
Avoidance of overworking	Praying and meditating	A pet animal
Fresh air and sunlight	Laughing	Avoid troublesome people
Decorating your home		Social service organizations
Hobbies		Reaching out to friends
A meaningful work life		
Sports and recreation		

Try this powerful practice: Give thanks for three things you usually take for granted. Do this just as you're preparing to drift off to sleep. Practice this for one week, and see what happens.

Meditation

If stress hampers your ability to handle conflict, you will be wise to consider daily meditation as a go-to conflict management strategy.

Meditation has been practiced in Eastern and Western cultures for thousands of years. Countless forms of meditation exist as part of many world religions.

Contrary to some popular beliefs, meditation doesn't necessarily need to be done sitting upright for long periods of time trying to 'empty the mind.' Meditation can be done through movement practices, such as yoga, T'ai Chi and many of the martial arts or through simply focusing on the breath and on what you feel in the present moment. Some say that running and swimming laps,

22

being repetitive activities, are forms of meditation. In fact, any proper activity - art, archery, pottery and woodworking, even house cleaning - that puts you in a calm, balanced state can be considered a meditation. The possibilities are practically endless.

In recent years, research has proved that a particular kind of meditation called **mindfulness meditation** improves mental and physical health. In mindfulness meditation you observe your present experience - your thoughts, emotions and sensations - with nonjudgmental curiosity. With practice, mindfulness meditation allows you to tune into the moment rather than obsessing over the past or the future. You can practice mindfulness meditation anywhere. Try it while you're washing dishes, feeling the soap and water run through your fingers, while standing in line at the grocery store, noticing what you're seeing, hearing and feeling. If waiting makes you feel impatient, this will help you.

Current studies on mindfulness meditation prove that it offers health benefits. Studies show that it reduces rumination (constant negative thoughts), significantly reduces stress, improves memory and focus, curbs emotional reactivity, sharpens the mind, improves sleep and increases immune functioning. Other studies suggest that a daily mindfulness meditation practice - which, again, you can do anytime, anywhere - promotes increased empathy and compassion, decreases symptoms of anxiety and depression, and leads to a better quality of life.

Here is a story which illustrates the power of meditation.

Many years ago I visited a friend who was living in a communal living group where life revolves around yoga and meditation. There, I met a woman whose story I remember to this day. She had been in a near-fatal auto accident. Her hips and legs were crushed so badly that her doctors said she would never walk again. Unwilling to accept that diagnosis, she turned to yoga and meditation. She made a full recovery and, despite the trauma of the accident, she appeared remarkably flexible and calm. Her recovery is just one of countless examples that illustrate the power of meditation and the healing power of the mind and body.

The Stress Response

When a conflict arises, we usually experience what is called the stress response. Our nervous system signals danger, and we go into a self-protective mode known as fight, flight or freeze.

This reaction involves the whole being - mind, body, emotions and actions. And, it shows up in any number of ways. We might threaten others, flee the scene, try to appease the instigator, minimize, joke or create distractions. This all-consuming state blocks communication and sensitivity to others, and then it's impossible to address conflict at all.

Understanding Conflict And Fight, Flight, Freeze

When conflict arises do you fight, flee or freeze up?

If you fight, do you …
Lash out verbally?
Get physical?
Use sarcasm?
Plot your revenge?
Involve other people as allies?
Demand that your opponent says "Uncle"?
Turn it around on another person?

If you flee, do you …
Use faulty logic to win an argument?
Minimize or make light of the problem?
Ignore the problem?
Distract yourself with a task?
Distract the other person with a non-issue?
Make up a story about the conflict to confuse the other person, causing him or her to question his/herself? This is called gaslighting.
Use so-called 'expert' language to prove the other person wrong or ignorant, trying to make the other person admit defeat? This seems like fighting, but it's actually a way of avoiding the real problem.
Try to help everyone get along without actually addressing the problem?
Over-sleep?
Use distractions, such as video games, social media, substances, shopping or food, for example, to avoid the problem?

And then, there's freezing.

If you freeze, do you …
Experience mental paralysis?
Experience significant confusion?
Not know what to do or say?

If any of these fight, flight or freeze responses happens to you, be reassured. The stress response need not be permanent. The information that follows can help you reach a calm, balanced state.

Then, when you realize that conflict does not always mean you're about to feel bad, you will be much less likely to avoid it. Rather, you will face it with confidence and readiness.

The Relaxation Response And The Vagus Nerve
When you apply the skills and ideas in this book, you will
tap into the thing that neutralizes the stress response - that
is, the relaxation response. It was Dr. Herbert Benson of
Harvard University's College of Medicine, who coined
the term in his wonderful book, *The Relaxation Response,*
which details how his research uncovered the many
benefits of transcendental meditation.

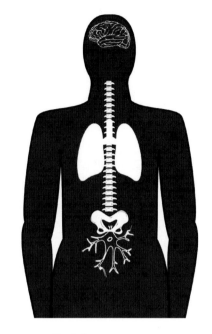

The relaxation response moves your mind-body state
away from self-protection (fight-flight-freeze) to a self-
regulated state of confidence and balance.

You may know that brain chemicals affect emotions and
mood. In this case we're referring to one specific
neurotransmitter chemical, acetylcholine, one of the
relaxation response brain chemicals. When we breathe
deeply and slowly, we stimulate an important part of the nervous system called the vagus nerve -
clearly, the diagram is not anatomically accurate, and is meant to give you an idea of the path it
takes - which regulates many of our unconscious processes, such as heartbeat, breathing and
digestion. The vagus nerve runs down the spinal column, and passes through the diaphragm.
When you breathe deeply, using the diaphragm, the vagus nerve is stimulated.

When the vagus nerve is stimulated, acetylcholine is released, prompting the relaxation response.
We activate the vagus nerve by taking deep, slow breaths, allowing the belly to move in and out.
You can find detailed information about the operation of the vagus nerve through many online
sources. By all means, educate yourself. And even more, prove for yourself what you feel, when
you activate the vagus nerve. The following exercise tells you how.

Breathing Exercise

Here's a simple exercise that stimulates the vagus nerve and activates the relaxation response. Do
this as part of your daily routine, and if you have time, before you enter a tense situation.

Lie on your back on the floor; knees bent and feet flat, so your legs form an upside down 'V.'
Place a book beneath your head. Position a cup or mug on your belly. Notice the cup's movement
as you breathe. Notice the calm feeling. After a minute or two, sit in a chair. Place one hand on
your chest and the other on your belly. Breathe as you did while lying down.
With regular practice, you will do this with ease. You will generally feel more and more relaxed.
You will also notice that when a conflict comes up, instead of jumping to the stress response,
your mind and body will go to the relaxation response.

You will also enjoy greater sharpened focus and clarity. You will see yourself as someone who is not controlled by outside factors and who can handle difficult situations. You will notice how your reaction to conflict is changing.

Prayer

Because much has been written about prayer, it seems presumptuous, not being a theologian, to add anything here. But consider this one idea. Praying to God keeps us connected to the Divine, the Eternal Good and reminds us that, no matter what happens in the world of humankind, there is another world for which we are destined, if we will reach out for it. One key idea: pray not for yourself, but for others, and relate to God with gratitude and humility. You may find the combination of prayer and meditation to be a most powerful stress reliever. And, as you may know, poorly managed stress blocks effective conflict resolution.

Goals

In Part 2, in addition to getting lots of tips, you'll be invited to take an honest look at yourself. If, as a result, you feel inspired to change your attitude or behavior, you will be wise to set clear goals. When you do so, three good things will happen. First, you will know exactly what you aim to change. Second, you will be able to track your progress. Third, you will be able to tell when you've attained your goal. Keep in mind that personal transformation is a life-long process, rather than the pursuit of an end result.

GOAL SETTING

"If you don't know where you are going, any road will get you there." - Lewis Carroll

Changes in old behaviors and attitudes may be necessary, and setting specific goals will be a great help. Interestingly, there is a right way to state a goal. It must be strong and clear, so that it gets you to adopt a new habit or attitude.

Your goal statement should be:

Specific and observable
Weak: "I want to get along better with my kids".
Strong: "I will spend at least 15 minutes with each of my kids every day having fun or teaching them something."

Detailed in terms of a new behavior, choice or action
Weak: "I am going to start exercising."
Strong: "I will join a local gym today, and go no fewer than four times a week, at least 30 minutes a visit."

Realistic and achievable
Weak: "I can be whatever I want to be."
Strong: "I will get training and education that fits my strengths and natural abilities, so that I'll always enjoy my work."

In your words and within your control
Weak: "I want my wife to stop nagging me."
Strong: "I will calm myself and think about my wife's own stresses, whenever she expresses frustration."

In the here and now; not 'some day'
Weak: "As soon as I get some money together, I'm moving to Hollywood to become a star."
Strong: "I will audition for 10 plays this year and continue taking acting and singing lessons every week for at least one year."

In positive terms - what you <u>will do</u> - not what you will stop doing.
Weak: "I'm going to quit smoking ."
Strong: "To resist the cravings, I will find a healthy way to get the relaxation that cigarettes used to provide."

PART 2

The "How To" of Conflict Resolution

Communication

"It's very hard to find your own words -
and you don't actually exist until you have your own words."
Jordan Peterson, Psychologist

"We don't communicate." Every couple says it. It's true and it's not true.

The reason is this: *you cannot not communicate*. That is one of the first principles I learned in my training as a therapist. Everything we do or don't do is a form of communication, whether it's deliberate or not. Here, the focus is on intentional communication.

Effective communication requires self-expression, which in turn requires understanding, skill and courage. That is, the courage to risk opening yourself up to rejection or some other kind of hurt. No wonder so many people hesitate to express emotions. They hide their thoughts and feelings or lie about them, which widens separation from others.

Let's examine some of the reasons people can't express themselves. Notice that all these reasons are related to anxiety - the worry about bad things that 'could' happen.

Embarrassment
Negative expectations about the outcome
Lack of trust in others
Early childhood training to not call attention to oneself
Fear of being judged or criticized
Fear of people knowing you better … because if they did, they might not like you
Inability to identify and/or verbalize feelings
There's no one to talk to
Nobody would listen, anyway
It's rude to talk about yourself
It's nobody's business
Reluctance to burden other people with your problems

If any of these apply to you, and the idea of changing strikes terror in your heart, take a breath. A personality makeover is not required. What is required is knowledge and skills. The following sections - in addition to the skills in Part 1 - will help you acquire the knowledge.

The benefits are immediately apparent. Showing your real self builds bridges to others and inspires them to open up in return.

After reading the following sections on Validation, Empathy and Observation and beginning to use the five skills from Part 1, you'll experience what I mean.

More on Communication and Listening

"I'm always willing to listen to advice, as long as it doesn't interfere with my plans."

When clients say they don't communicate, I ask what communication means to them. Is it casual conversation? Is it an attempt to talk about opinions or feelings? Is it about sharing an activity without talking? Is it a touch? A gesture?

Effective communication occurs when the receiver gets the message just as the sender intended. This rarely happens when the receiver's attention has been derailed by what we call a "trigger." The trigger creates interfering noise in the mind - negative, self-defeating or hostile self-talk - and listening stops.

You have probably experienced one unintended consequence of being triggered: you not only stop listening, but you also prepare your answer. The 5-Second Rule solves this problem by making you wait calmly.

Now, what if the other person says something that irritates or offends you? Your immediate impulse is to defend yourself or to prove the other person wrong. Unfortunately, a defensive reaction rarely helps. If you're offended and might forget your intended reply, jot it down and wait. Meanwhile, use STOP - BREATHE - RE-THINK.

Take that deep breath, and be calm before talking. Then - and this is just as important - if you start feeling agitated, refer back to the skills in Part 1 to restore inner calm. It's easier than you might think.

Now, about this listening thing … We've all heard, 'He doesn't listen.' Or, 'She just hears what she wants to hear.' The fact is that most people don't really listen, especially when they're fussing and feuding. Consider the following actual case.

Frankie and Johnny are good, decent people, married with two children. They both work full-time. During her childhood Frankie was bullied by other girls, and her mother belittled and criticized her severely. She developed anxiety and a high degree of sensitivity to criticism. As a result, she doesn't like it when she wants to do something, and Johnny tells her no. They love each other, but they argue a lot, usually over money. When they argue - sometimes because Frankie wants to buy something pricey, Johnny says no and criticizes her. The moment that happens, Frankie no longer hears his voice. Rather, she hears her mother's negative, angry voice. She either shuts down or becomes defiant.

People who have been abused often react this way. When stress builds up, traumatic memories can activate the fight-flight stress hormones, and fear takes over. In this mind-body state, communication is impossible, because we are no longer paying attention to the present.

In order to handle conflict effectively, become a good listener. That means being tuned-in to the other person's needs and feelings. This is only possible when the noise in your mind fades into the background as a result of your using the skills in Part 1.

If your handling of conflict is hampered because your fear or anger are quickly triggered, a well-trained therapist can help you neutralize the impact of painful memories, so that you are free to respond to what's happening in the moment. By learning how to stay present, a whole new world opens up to you.

Validation

"So encourage one another and build each other up, just as in fact you are doing."
1 Thessalonians 5:11

Have you ever dismissed, rejected or criticized the feelings of a spouse, partner, child or friend? If so, and the conflict didn't get resolved, don't blame the other person. Your actions prompted the other person to put up a wall.

Consider George and Martha, a young couple with a history of conflict with George's businessman father, Jedediah. Jedediah and Priscilla had been married for thirty-five years. Priscilla was submissive and Jedediah was dominant. Jedediah did not respect George as an adult, and always told him how to do this and that. After years of this, George and Martha stopped seeing Jedediah and Priscilla for a year. That included no contact with the grandchildren.

While I worked primarily with the young couple, George's parents attended a couple of sessions. Clearly, Jedediah portrayed himself as the 'expert', while Priscilla said nothing, but cried a lot. At one point, Jedediah disagreed with George when George said he had always felt put down by his dad. The dad's words still ring in my ears: "You have no reason to feel like that. You shouldn't feel like that. Am I wrong?" In vain, he turned to me for support.

Denying a person's feelings is extremely disrespectful and sometimes, downright hostile. No one should have to defend their emotions, because emotions are not subject to logic or reason. They just are. Using the word "should" is like trying to jam a square peg into a round hole. Emotions and opinions are two different mental activities, and they don't mix.

Sadly, that kind of language is common during conflicts. If that's you, you can decide right now to change your judgmental mindset and learn to treat people with sensitivity and respect. Start by using The Reflecting Statement in Part 1.

Empathy

"Never criticize a man until you've walked a mile in his moccasins." - Native American proverb

Empathy is the capacity to identify with and to experience another person's feelings. This ability will go a long way to greasing the wheels of conflict resolution. Lacking that sensitivity, you might not validate the other person. This communicates that you don't care how she feels. So, here's a question. If you're not naturally tuned into other people's feelings, can you learn?

During the 1960's Civil Rights movement, a man named George Wallace was Governor of Alabama. His vigorous opposition to school integration appeared to show that he cared only about white people. One day he was shot, and spent his remaining years in a wheelchair. As his life was changed, so was his mind. He dropped his apparent hatred of black people and his attempts to deprive them of their rights.

If you believe that a hard heart can be softened … if you believe that empathy can be learned … that people can learn to understand and care about others, rather than seeing them as non-persons … how might that happen?

You might begin by changing the way you perceive people. You can learn to read body language, and you can ask directly about what another person needs and is feeling. Once you've acquired that new habit, your observation skills might improve dramatically, and you might even learn to trust your gut feeling. That could be a game-changer.

Observation

"You can observe a lot just by watching." - Yogi Berra, U. S. Baseball Hall of Fame

During an argument, body language speaks much louder than words do. Thus, understanding body language is extremely important. Think about it. Hasn't an eye-roll, a snort or dirty look ever pushed your button?

Body language encompasses the following behaviors:

Tone of voice
Facial expressions and behaviors
Physical position in relation to yours
Gestures
Posture
General demeanor; relaxed or tense
Personal grooming and choice of clothing
The pace of speech
The speed of response when in conversation
Promptness
Breathing patterns
Skin tone
Foot movements
Shoulder height, sitting posture

It is wise to learn to read people's emotions. But be aware that others may be observing you, as well. Even without watching or listening closely, they might sense what you're communicating, while you don't know you're doing it. For example, unhappy parents might not see that the kids know when mom and dad are at odds, even if they're not arguing.

Here's a real case proving that you can become aware of the signals you send unconsciously.

A female client of mine once said that when she and her husband dined out, he looked at every woman who walked by. He was doing so unconsciously, not knowing that it hurt her feelings. His lack of self-awareness rendered him unaware of his own body language. Fortunately, as she patiently called this behavior to his attention, he made a conscious effort to notice the habit and to change it.

The good news is that most people can learn to interpret body language fairly well. And, with a little help from their friends, they can learn to be aware of their own body language. Ask for help from someone you trust. Tell her you want to learn to understand body language. Go out in public together, and have fun observing people at random. Talk about the expressions you see on people's faces, their clothing, their postures and their ways of talking. That includes the volume, pace and pitch of their speech and tone of voice. Notice how your impressions of other people's behavior compares to your friend's impressions. In this way you can enjoy yourselves while you're learning.

Understanding your own body language and correctly interpreting the body language of others will enhance your ability to handle conflict. Don't wait till 'some day'. Set a goal using the guidelines in Part 1, and watch what happens.

Triggers

"A fool can only learn from his own mistakes.
But a wise man learns from the mistakes of others." - Otto von Bismarck

A trigger in this sense refers to a behavior or a thought - from your environment, from other people, or from within your own mind - which provokes a knee-jerk reaction.

A therapist was working with a troubled young woman who had been sexually assaulted and suffered for years afterward. Despite his sincerest efforts, he was not able to encourage the client to talk about the trauma. It seemed that she didn't trust him.

Ultimately, after some time, the therapist succeeded in having the client describe the sights, sounds and smells connected to the trauma. She said one thing stood out: the perpetrator used a specific brand of after-shave lotion. This was the 'Aha!' moment. The therapist had been using the same brand himself. Each time she met with him, she was being triggered without knowing it. This was probably because a scent on one person's skin can differ from that scent on another person. She never identified the scent on the therapist, but beneath the level of consciousness, she was still triggered.

If you tend to be easily triggered during conflict, try the following:

> List your triggers - internal and external - that prevent you from addressing
> conflict effectively.
> List the physical feelings that warn you that you've been triggered. These feelings are
> warning signs, alerting you that you've been triggered.
> If you feel triggered, use the STOP - BREATHE - RE-THINK skill
> from Part 1.

If you are easily triggered in general, you will be wise to examine your lifestyle, review the Long-Term Approach in Part 1 and consider adopting some new health-giving habits.

See p. 44, "Your Inner Language". It connects very well with this section.

The Blinding Effect of Self-Focus

"I once was lost, but now am found. Was blind, but now I see."
Amazing Grace

We are wise to understand our triggers and, when negative emotions are triggered, to have the ability to restore balance and clear thinking.

The difficulty is that, when we are stressed, we focus on one thing only: our own safety, our feelings, our fears. We lose sight of the big picture. We lose the ability to feel for the other person. We can become insensitive and uncaring.

As in tunnel vision, we lose perspective. We only sense the current threat - real or imagined - and we overemphasize its importance. We make mountains out of molehills and we fight battles that don't need to be fought.

A loss of perspective can happen to anyone. But it doesn't have to be that way for the rest of your life.

When you're embroiled in a relationship conflict, use the STOP - BREATHE - RETHINK skill from Part 1 in order to regain access to your reasoning brain. Use the Limited Time Out, if necessary. After regaining a feeling of calm and balance, you can ask yourself how much this really matters in the long run. In one year, two years, five years … will I look back at this and ask myself, what was I thinking?

Start with a Positive Statement or Question

"But the fruit of the Spirit is love, joy, peace, patience,
kindness, goodness, faithfulness, gentleness, self-control…" - Galatians 5:22-23

The person who possesses wisdom and maturity respects the rights and needs of all people, and shows it by his behavior and attitude.

When world leaders get together to iron out disagreements, the wise leader begins by acknowledging the strengths of both parties and the bond between them, based on common values, goals and interests.

This is not merely a matter of courtesy or protocol. It's practical. In resolving conflicts, starting with negativity or harshness guarantees failure.

Before trying to resolve a relationship problem, set a positive tone. Find common ground. This creates a spirit of cooperation, rather than competition.

Start by asking a question that will get a 'yes' answer. For example, you might say something like, "I believe we have a problem. Would you agree?" or … "This has been hard for all of us, hasn't it?" And then, "I'd like to get this resolved; wouldn't you?" or, "I'm ready to work this out; will you help me?" By obtaining at least one 'yes', you've created a mood of cooperation and hope. Instead of approaching each other as adversaries, you can act as allies.

In some cases the other party may deny the problem. As in, 'I don't have a problem. You have a problem.' In such a case you can decide what this relationship means to you. Can you set limits on this person's ability to affect you? This would be a good time to learn about boundaries in relationship. If you have not heard about boundaries in personal relationships, you would be wise to educate yourself. Go to your local book store or online source, and look for books about boundaries. Many of them are available in audible versions. I strongly recommend *Boundaries: When to Say Yes, How to Say No, To Take Control of Your Life* by Cloud and Townsend.

Name the Conflict

"If I had one hour to solve a problem, I would spend fifty-five minutes thinking about the problem and five minutes thinking about solutions." - Albert Einstein

Start on a positive note … achieve a calm mood … obtain at least one agreement. That's all good stuff. And identifying the conflict accurately is equally important. This takes some thought.

To illustrate:

Stanley and Stella plan a vacation with their kids. Stanley insists on playing golf. Stella has her heart set on a beach vacation. The kids are begging to go to an amusement park. They argue and get nowhere. But what is the actual conflict? It's not just that they disagree. The actual conflict is that none of them will compromise. That is the thing that needs to change.

While poor communication is a genuine issue, it's usually a symptom of deeper problems. When people in conflict cite communication as the problem, that's just the tip of the iceberg. Beneath the surface there may be a powerful back story. She may be afraid to give an inch because she was raised by abusive alcoholics who never let her express herself. Or, he was raised by old-school parents who believed that dad always had the last word.

Avoid dwelling on the stuff you're arguing about. Do not get into 'he said-she said' arguments.

Instead, focus on the way you're communicating. Be aware of your tendency to interrupt, react too fast, shut down, criticize, pile one complaint on top of another, and so on. In Part 3, see *The Rules of Engagement Questionnaire*. If you use it, it will help you greatly.

The rest of this book will give you many useful tools and ideas.

Check Yourself, First

"Why do you see the speck that is in your brother's eye, but do not notice the log that is in your own eye? Or how can you say to your brother, 'Let me take the speck out of your eye,' when there is the log in your own eye? You hypocrite, first take the log out of your own eye, and then you will see clearly to take the speck out of your brother's eye." - Matthew 7: 3-5

During a training class on crisis management, my colleagues and I viewed a video which recorded a real time event, which illustrated how not to handle a problem.

The setting: an inner city high school office area. The time: the end of a school day. A teacher, angry about the many absences of one student, called the teen to his office. Looking more adult than schoolboy, the student entered, scowling. Before anything else, the teacher lit into this kid about his absences. The student talked back and instantly a verbal and physical fight broke out. The police were called and the kid was led off in cuffs.

Consider two important lessons regarding crisis management, which also apply to conflict resolution:

#1: When entering a tense situation, the first thing to do is to check the scene for danger.

#2: Check yourself. Do not try to defuse an explosive situation if you feel so tense that you could be triggered. Note that the teacher in this video had already been triggered. Thus, he adopted a dominant position with the teen, which ruined his chance of influencing this young man.

In addressing a conflict, check what you're feeling emotionally and physically before you speak. When emotion is in charge of you or the other person, wait. Use the Limited Time-Out as explained in Part 1.

Daily practice in relaxation and staying in the moment will help you train yourself to maintain a sense of calm and balance through your day. The goal is to train yourself to be less reactive to stressful situations.

As for the student, here's the rest of the story. He was eighteen, and a senior. His mother, a single mom, unable to work, stayed home to care for the little ones. This young man was working full time to support the family. If the teacher had been aware of his own outrage, brought himself under control and gotten the full picture, he might have been able to think clearly and identify the real problem.

Do Not Assume

"You, therefore, have no excuse, you who pass judgment on someone else, for at whatever point you judge another, you are condemning yourself, because you who pass judgment do the same things." - Romans 2: 1-3

A middle-aged client is unhappy and confused, because his wife wants to divorce him. He says, "I don't know what she thinks about the fact that I work with this pretty woman. I don't know - she might be mad about something else. I assume she's jealous and she wants me to find another job." That's the short version.

These people have been married for nearly twenty years, and he still assumes he knows what she is thinking.

When we assume we know the negative thoughts, feelings or motives of another, we immediately jump to conclusions. We take things personally, we're often wrong, and we say or do something that makes matters worse.

If this applies to you, rather than taking things personally and jumping to conclusions, simply ask the other person whether you understood her correctly. If you're reluctant to speak in such a direct manner, what are you assuming? That the direct approach is offensive? How do you know if that's really true? Do you assume you can read people's minds? How many assumptions can you pile on top of the others?

The direct approach is usually best. It eliminates the confusion of guessing and misunderstanding. It's not always easy, but with a little coaching, anyone can learn to address conflict this way. For more ideas about this, check out the section called Assertive vs. Aggressive.

Your Inner Language

"You will never be free until you free yourself
from the prison of your own false thoughts." - Anonymous

This section builds upon the one just before it and addresses a major obstacle to conflict resolution. The obstacle contains three parts.

First, assuming you know what others think, feel, or intend.
Second, assuming you know the reasons for their behavior.
Third, verbalizing your assumptions.

When we assume wrongly, expressing that assumption provokes defensiveness. Communication comes to a halt, and you lose the chance to resolve the conflict.

Now, let's go deeper. We all have the tendency to assume; and our assumptions are a result of beliefs stored in our memory - beliefs about life, about ourselves, the world, people, and so on. These long-held beliefs profoundly influence our major life decisions, our relationships and our way of coping with stress and conflict. Further, these beliefs find expression in random thoughts throughout the day.

Our moment-to-moment thoughts also affect the way we handle conflict. In the geeky language of therapy, we refer to these thoughts as our "self-talk."

Most self-talk takes place as if it has a life of its own. It happens automatically, like a knee-jerk reflex. Self-talk can help us think positively, or it can do the opposite.

Here's an example. A client told me that her way to relieve stress is to go shopping. She also said she's put on a lot of weight, and she really "needs" to start exercising. As we talked, she realized she could exercise in place of shopping. Her words were, I could "make myself" go to the gym. She spoke this out loud, but this is the kind of thing we do in our silent self-talk as well. Remember, the language we use when we talk to ourselves has a powerful effect on our choices and feelings.

If you have to make yourself go to the gym, will you be motivated to do it? Or will you resent it? When I asked her that, she laughed and said, "Oh, geez, that sounds like a chore." Then she realized that she could use different words - words with a positive spin - to motivate her to exercise. For instance, 'I'd like to go to the gym to do the kind of activity I could do easily, and do just enough that I'd gladly do it again.'

You see the positive words in that last sentence (notice that the word 'exercise' was not used)? This is the kind of positive self-talk that can help anyone achieve his or her goals.

The next time you are faced with a relationship conflict, notice the self-talk that your mind does AUTOMATICALLY and INSTANTLY. If it's negative - like, 'Oh no, do I really have to deal with this again!?' or anything else that means you're expecting trouble, remember one of your new tools: STOP - BREATHE - RE-THINK

Stop that thought right away.

Take a deep breath.

CHOOSE a different thought. A thought that will help you approach the conflict with a positive attitude and a statement of cooperation.

Some samples of positive thoughts you might use in place of the negative, 'Oh, no!' thoughts:

'If I handle this well, this could be a learning experience.'
'I am probably no better at handling conflict than (s)he is, so I'll tread lightly.'
'If I get this right, this would be a good example for my co-workers.'
'I believe I can get through this if I show the other person that I am willing to hang in.'
'If I handle this well with my kids, I will earn even more of my spouse's respect.'
'I know that I can handle this if I stay calm and keep breathing evenly and deeply.'

Because negative thinking is automatic and instant, virtually everyone should regularly practice using positive words in the face of conflicts.

"I Know What You Want"

"Do not scheme against each other. Stop your love of telling lies that you swear are the truth. I hate all these things, says the LORD."." - Zechariah 8:17

Once again, notice that the main idea in this chapter builds upon the previous one.

In all wars, a major objective is to understand the enemy's strategy. What are they trying to do? How can we stop them? This is how we think when we see the other person as 'the enemy.'

Notice the language you use when you argue. Do you ever try to define the other person's motives? Have you ever said anything like, "You're just trying to _____." Or, "All you care about is _____." Or, "I know what you want, it's the same thing all over again." "You're not fooling me. I know what you're up to." Or, "Sure, you might change for a week or two, and then you'll go back to your old self." If you have talked like that, how did the other person react?

Think back to a situation when you were on the receiving end of that disrespectful speech. How did it feel to have someone claim to know what you're thinking, planning and scheming? How did you react?

NEVER claim to 'know' the other person's motives. This is a huge no-no. When you do that, the other person reacts defensively, communication is over and the conflict can escalate in a heartbeat. If you must know what's motivating the other person, be direct and ask respectfully.

In talking through a conflict, if the other person reacts defensively, ask yourself whether you did or said something to trigger him or her. Better yet, ask the other person.

Address the other person as an ally or partner - as someone who can help you work out the problem. Enlist his aid, ask her advice and notice how differently that turns out.

Projection

Projection is a form of defense in which unwanted feelings are displaced onto another person, where they then appear as a threat from the external world.
A paraphrase from the works of Sigmund Freud

Years ago I helped chaperone a group of college students on a visit to a Hindu temple. Most of them had no familiarity with people of different cultures. So, in this strange, exotic space permeated with the aroma of incense, soft, dim lighting, people dressed in colorful native garb and alcoves in each of the walls, containing shrines and offerings to Hindu gods, the reactions of the students ranged from wonder to confusion to genuine curiosity. After the visit I heard one of them say, "It's amazing to think that these people are just as strong in their beliefs as we are in ours."

How do you cope with people who think and believe differently from the way you do?

Are you self-confident? Do you respect yourself, while accepting there's always room for improvement? If so, you probably have no problem with others' differences. On the contrary, the insecure personality needs others to approve of them, to agree with them and to share their tastes and preferences.

Do you assume that your child, spouse or partner is like you? That is projection. We project our personalities, our beliefs, feelings and tastes onto others.

Imagine a couple, Brad and Scarlett. Brad loves a massage when he's tense. He loves hugs and pats on the back. Scarlett does not. She's touchy about being touched. Brad assumes that she is like him. After all, 'Who doesn't love a massage?' So, when he senses she's stressed, he gently rubs her shoulder. She flinches and tells him to stop. He's confused and wonders what's wrong with her. She's offended by his insensitivity. If the pattern continues, he may stop giving her affection of any kind. Then she'll feel rejected. And so it might go, round and round.

You can learn to stop projecting and, instead, appreciate other people's differences by reading Gary Chapman's wonderful book, *The 5 Love Languages*. It explains that each individual experiences being loved in his or her unique way.

Lend a Hand

"Two are better than one, because they have a good reward for their toil. For if they fall, one will lift up his fellow; but woe to him who is alone when he falls and has not another to lift him up. Again, if two lie together, they are warm; but how can one be warm alone? And though a man might prevail against one who is alone, two will withstand him. A threefold cord is not quickly broken." - Ecclesiastes 4: 9-12

Improving your way of handling conflict may require changes to thinking, attitudes and behavior. In line with that statement, please keep this principle in mind:

Personal transformation is impossible without positive feedback.

Imagine a student, struggling in algebra. Your parents tell you to work harder. You do so, and you get an A. Wonderful! But, what if your parents do not acknowledge your efforts with words of praise, or some other kind of reward? Will you be motivated to keep up the good work?

Conflicts can be exhausting, and both participants need relief. Each one blames the other, and might say, "I'm not changing until you do something about _____." Neither one will budge.

Fortunately, a solution exists. But you must be willing to acknowledge the other person's small improvements. Giving appreciation of the smallest of changes is absolutely critical.

Use *The Rules of Engagement Questionnaire* in Part 3 to select the habits you wish to change. Review your goals and track your progress. When you notice the other person improving, even a little bit, praise it. Reinforce it. Help the other person to repeat that new habit.

When your spouse, child or partner makes a positive change, reward her in a way that she truly appreciates. Don't assume she likes the same things you do. If she's not materialistic, don't buy her a gift. If she simply likes to spend time together, give her your time. When you give words of praise or do something nice for her, you might see the gratitude in her eyes or hear it in her voice. Or maybe she just wants a hug. The moment you begin doing this, you will see your relationship blossom.

Unfortunately, this may not always work out. In fact, some people, mainly men, would praise their children, their softball teammates or co-workers. But praise their spouse or partner for changing a bad habit? They won't do it. To them, that's nothing more than coddling, and adults don't need to be coddled. That is a problem, and in my experience, people who hold that belief are not likely to give it up. This is the kind of thing that should be spotted before entering a committed relationship.

A Tip for Blended Families

"Rules minus relationship equals rebellion." - Josh McDowell, Author and Minister

Blended families have their own unique sets of problems. One of the most common is that the step-parent attempts to exercise authority over the spouse's children without having formed a bond of affection, respect and trust.

A client of mine, an educated professional woman named Laura, told me that her husband, Rob, made this mistake in a big way. Rob and one of her two teenage sons got into a minor physical altercation, which led to her calling the police. More problems ensued between Rob and the boys, and it became clear that this marriage was a mistake.

Since I had met them in couples sessions before they married, his attitude showed that he was not suited to be in a close relationship of any kind. In fact, his behavior and attitude reeked of narcissism. Despite noting his negative traits, Laura married him several months later. At the time she returned for counseling, she had begun to wonder if she should leave him.

If you're a step-parent, don't make the same mistakes that Rob made. Regardless of your upbringing, your values, your style of parenting and your beliefs about who runs the family, never try to exert authority over your step-children—until and unless they clearly show that they care for you and trust you. Never apply consequences without consulting the biological parent. Some exceptions do exist, of course. But in general, if you follow this principle, you'll experience much less frustration and conflict.

Incidentally, Laura filed for divorce about one year after the wedding.

Respect

"Do not repay evil with evil or insult with insult. On the contrary, repay evil with blessing, because to this you were called so that you may inherit a blessing." - 1 Peter 3: 9

During my many years as a therapist and program director at a treatment center for teens, nearly all the kids said the same thing about respect: "You respect me before I respect you."

If everyone followed that belief, we'd all be waiting for others to respect us first.

But, before we criticize the teenagers, consider one important truth. All the kids in that program were trauma victims. All had been subject to extreme forms of disrespect, such as abuse and neglect. Of course they demanded respect first. They didn't trust anyone.

What do you think about when you think of respect? Do you think that respect must be earned? And yet, do you believe that everyone deserves to be respected?

That makes no sense, unless we consider the possibility that respect is not just one thing. And that's a fact. Respect is more than just one thing.

First, every person has the right to basic respect. Eastern religions and Native American cultures believe that all life is sacred and must be respected, down to the tiny bug and the lowly weed.

Second, the respect that we owe to family, just because they're part of our blood line. As the saying goes, one definition of family is, 'when you knock on their door, they have to let you in.'

Third, the respect we give to appointed or elected public officials or religious figures.

Fourth, the respect we give to authority figures: parents, teachers, coaches.

Fifth, the respect given to genuine heroes who risk and sacrifice for the good of others.

Sixth, people who have fought through life's storms.

Seventh, people with special gifts and talents. Geniuses who go the extra mile to benefit mankind.

When you are in conflict, who owes respect to whom? And when you're talking to the other person, ask yourself how you would respond if (s)he talked to you that way.

Assertive vs. Aggressive

"After you've cut off a person's nose, there's no point giving her flowers." - Ancient proverb

A lovely, thoughtful lady, well past retirement age, came to me for therapy. Even in this season of her life, she wished to improve herself. She explained she'd always had difficulty speaking up.

In early childhood, she was taught that speaking up was rude. She was told to be quiet, to keep her thoughts to herself and not to bother people with her problems. She also believed that speaking up would make people angry with her.

After many years as a therapist, I've noticed that people who have trouble speaking up confuse assertiveness with aggression. They assume that if they speak up, others will think they're picking a fight. So, they develop a fear of voicing legitimate complaints.

There are no hard rules about this. Sometimes speaking up is the right thing, and sometimes it's not. But this exercise can help.

Ask your spouse, partner or child to do this activity together. On a scale from 1 - 10, with 10 being highest, rate your ability to judge when it's best to speak or not to speak in any given situation. This is a critical thinking skill and social skill.

Now, to help you become brave enough to speak up, ask yourself: 'What are the negative thoughts and beliefs that go with my fear of speaking up?' Then, ask yourself 'What would I prefer to believe about that?' Write it down, and when you go to bed, begin to think about what you prefer to believe, as you're drifting off to sleep.

If your inability to speak up is affecting your happiness, it may be time to consult a professional.

Power and Status

"All animals are created equal. But some animals are more equal than others."
from *Animal Farm* by George Orwell

Every human relationship contains elements of power and status. One person is on top, the other is on the bottom.

If you've watched *A Christmas Story*, the movie about Ralphie's dream of owning a super-duper air rifle, you know the scene in which Ralphie beats up the bully, Farkas. This moment comes as a huge shock to both boys. The powerful message in this vignette is that Farkas has pushed Ralphie to the limits of his ability to tolerate the bullying. It's as though a light bulb goes on in Ralphie's head and he senses that he must do something. And does he ever! What's also fascinating is that, after Ralphie has bloodied Farkas's nose and Farkas is crying, Ralphie's mom rushes in, pulls Ralphie away, and, as Farkas exits the scene, Ralphie breaks down in tears.

When you're at odds with someone, what is most important to you? To avoid? To win at all costs? To please the other person? To not make things worse? To make light of it? To get one over on the other person?

If we lived in The Garden of Eden, we'd have no need to overpower others. We'd be equals, living in peace and harmony. Unfortunately, Planet Earth is not all garden; it's partly jungle. Conflicts arise, and sometimes we are forced to respond. The way we respond depends partly on how we see ourselves compared to others.

Now, back to Ralphie. Bullies dominate until they meet someone who appears more powerful. In a burst of raw emotion, Ralphie suddenly realized he had power, and he taught Farkas a lesson.

So often we feel like losers when we're in conflict. Consumed with fear, we believe we have no power. If that pattern is repeated, we begin to incorporate the loser label into our identity. In such a case, morphing into a winner is a much greater challenge.

But what if you no longer viewed conflict as a power struggle, but rather as an opportunity to accomplish something good? What if you could find a way to promote equality between the parties in the conflict? No status difference; no big fish and little fish.

The next time you face a relationship conflict, ask yourself if the other person really is more powerful than you are. Or am I yielding power, because I'm afraid?" What can I do to move this away from a power struggle to something productive?

When you think that way, you will not react emotionally and your adult mind will be free to look for solutions.

Stay Focused

"I don't care how much power, brilliance or energy you have. If you don't harness it and focus it on a specific target, and hold it there, you're never going to accomplish as much as your ability warrants." - Zig Ziglar, Author

A couple comes for counseling, and they say, "We talk and talk, and don't get anywhere. We always end up where we started. It's so frustrating!" Has this ever happened in your relationship? For couples and families who experience constant conflict, it's a common complaint.

When trying to resolve a conflict, keep it simple. Address one thing at a time. Do not pile issue upon issue.

Use the 5-Second Rule explained in Part 1 to slow the communication down. Give the other person time to follow your thinking and time to respond. Slow and soften the pace and volume of your speech.

Do not stray from the topic. Going off on tangents is a waste of time and energy.

Do not dredge up the past. This is one of the most destructive things you can do when you're arguing. It indicates that you can't or won't let go. It makes you look and sound unforgiving and stubborn, and causes the other person to doubt your ability or willingness to make peace. If this toes on, you may lose the other person's trust completely.

If you happen to lose focus and start feeling agitated, stop talking. Use The Limited Time Out, described in Part 1. After you've regained focus, pick up the conversation again.

The Blame Game

"Love is patient and kind; love is not jealous or boastful; it is not arrogant or rude. Love does not insist on its own way; it is not irritable or resentful; it does not rejoice at wrong, but rejoices in the right. Love bears all things, believes all things, hopes all things, endures all things. Love never ends ..." - 1 Corinthians 13: 4-8

When you argue, do you and your spouse, partner or child tend to blame each other? Do you use words that label the other person, such as, 'you're selfish, you're lazy, you're stubborn', etc.? Back and forth it goes, and everyone gets frustrated.

Communication and conflict resolution are two-way streets. Everyone involved plays a role in creating and furthering conflicts, even if they're not the ones who created it in the first place. In order to break the cycle, all - with the exception of the very young - must come to accept that fact and take responsibility for their part.

When we blame and label others, we usually start by saying "you." As in, "You never do what you say you'll do ... you always turn it back on me", etc. If you start your sentence with "you", unless you're supporting the other person, you're going to get a defensive reaction. They attack, you defend. Communication is finished.

Fortunately, there is a way out of this cycle of mutual blame and labeling. It's the 'I' statement. If you haven't begun to use it, please go back to Part 1 and re-read it completely. It works. But it requires practice, practice, practice. If you don't quite get how and why it works, see "The I Statement Reloaded" in Part 3.

Differing Styles

"The only difference between the saint and the sinner is that every saint has a past, and every sinner has a future." - Oscar Wilde, Author and Playwright

Rarely do people think alike about problems. And it's equally rare for any two people to operate at the same pace. These differences are rooted in personality traits.

When trying to resolve a conflict, both people should acknowledge their differences, and accept that neither one is always right and neither way of addressing the conflict is always right.

Charlie and Mabel are in conflict. Mabel thinks more quickly than Charlie does. She wants to address issues right away and move on. But Charlie doesn't think as fast as Mabel does, and he needs time to ponder. Neither one is right or wrong.

Mabel might conclude that Charlie is avoiding the problem. That may be true., but it's also possible that he simply needs more time. If she rushes the process, he will feel pressured. If this pattern continues, both of them will fall into the cycle of mutual blame and labeling. This may lead to conflict avoidance, which, as you've read, is toxic for a relationship.

The good news is that there is a solution. For the solution to work, both people must agree to a new 'rule'.

When one of the them is not ready to talk, the other person agrees to give him or her the time he or she needs. The person who needs time agrees to do whatever it takes to address the problem, and states when they can pick up the conversation. Review The Limited Time-Out in Part 1.

If it's hard to accept that the other person does not always agree with you, think and act as you do, etc. - this would be a good time for you to take stock of yourself. That is to say, what is it about you that has difficulty tolerating the other person's differences?

Lying

"A verbal agreement isn't worth the paper it's written on."
Samuel Goldwyn, Film Producer

The obvious warnings - do not yell, curse, do not physically abuse, threaten, run away, etc. - are absent from this work. I believe you know enough to avoid such behaviors.

What about lying? We all know that honesty is essential to building trust. And yet, don't some of us lie, sometimes? Even a little white lie?

Before we go further, let's be clear about what constitutes a lie. Is it just a matter of deliberately stating a falsehood? Or, is there more to it? Please consider some additional ways of lying:

Leaving out information
Not saying how you really feel
Twisting words in order to fool or mislead the other person
Masking your appearance or image for personal advantage

Briefly, any action intended to deceive is a lie. This includes deceiving oneself. More on that, later.

A client of mine, Cheryl, is upset because her adult sister, Emma, has lied to her on many occasions. Cheryl says she can't trust Emma anymore. Working with Cheryl, we acknowledged the varied reasons that people lie. Among them:

To avoid blame or punishment
To advance one's agenda
To hurt others
To deflect attention
To keep people from getting too close
To prevent a disaster
To protect another person
Because of a feeling of shame and guilt

Cheryl realized that Emma had been lying, not in order to hurt her, but out of shame. Cheryl then described Emma's chaotic life. An unfaithful husband, kids out of control, and more. Once Cheryl realized that she had assumed the motive for Emma's lying, she was able to understand the deeper problem.

Now, back to lying to oneself. Consider one way we do that: we deny our feelings. This form of dishonesty obstructs conflict resolution. Compare it to the Assertive vs Aggressive chapter.

Typically, lying to oneself stems from fear of conflict, fear of rejection, and self-doubt. It is generally rooted in early life experiences, possibly traumatic episodes or the memories of a dysfunctional family life.

If this is a problem for you, first of all, identify the fear behind your lie: fear of criticism, judgment, fear of being left out and isolated, etc. Is your fear justifiable by evidence? Are you holding on to fears from long ago, which no longer serve any function?

When you voice your fear directly to the other person, you may find that overcoming it is not as hard as you imagined. The other person will be wise to respect your feelings, to validate your fear and may even be able to help you to let go of it. However, in some cases professional help is indicated. See the last section in Part 2, "Be Wise When You Share."

The Internal Struggle

"Every kingdom divided against itself is brought to desolation, and every city or house divided against itself will not stand." - Matthew 12: 25

Imagine two people, Jason and Justin, each with different life situations.

Jason hates his job. He struggles financially. His personal life is a mess.

Justin has a passion for his profession, is financially stable and loves his family.

Jason wanted to be an artist, knowing it might offer no guarantee of financial stability. His family pressured him to take the safe route. He reluctantly agreed, graduated from business school, works in a high-rise office building, and hates what he's doing. He feels like a coward and a failure.

Justin was allowed the freedom to pursue his dreams, and is enjoying a sense of wholeness and fulfillment.

Jason has ongoing conflicts with co-workers and others.

Justin is at peace with himself, is comfortable in his own skin and rarely has conflicts with other people.

Jason's internal struggle has created an ongoing negative state of mind. It has damaged his opinion of himself and of his family, and the damage shows up in the way he behaves with others.

You may know someone like Jason. He is, as an old saying goes, "A nation at war with itself."

If you're having trouble resolving conflicts and you're not sure why, ask yourself what you're struggling with inside. Are you caught between what you want, versus what other people say you should do? Have you created your own trap by not being honest with yourself? And finally, the question which addresses the source of these problems, "What are you afraid of?"

Naming the internal struggle may be your first step in finding peace. That is, a peace that begins with accepting reality - rather than insisting that things should have turned out otherwise - and treating yourself with respect and compassion. When you achieve that inner peace, you will be ready to relate to others with compassion and understanding.

Unrealistic Expectations

"Women marry men, hoping that they will change.
Men marry women, hoping that they won't."

Successful conflict resolution depends largely on our expectations.

Expectations are ingrained in our minds from early childhood, and continue into adulthood. In pre-school we expect an order of activities: play time, milk and cookies, nap time and pick up time. Adults expect hard work to be rewarded. We expect family to be loving, friends to be loyal, first responders to be brave.

The wise person bases his or her expectations on solid foundations, such as the law, a written contract or long experience with a trusted individual or organization. But the person lacking in wisdom relies on changeable factors, such as rumors, the weather and the stock market.

If you base your expectations on …

> The behavior, speech and moods of others
> Your employer's policies, rules and regulations
> Educational and religious institutions
> The behavior of politicians
> The behavior of the press and other media
> The conduct of self-described moral role models, such as religious leaders

… you might find yourself severely disappointed, at the very least.

All the above are subject to change at any time.

We also make a mistake if we base our expectations on what is 'supposed' to happen in an ideal world. Expectations should be based on what is really happening, rather than what's supposed to happen or what we wish would happen.

Some idealistic beliefs and expectations, which, when busted, might rock your world:

> 'If he really loves me, he should understand what I'm feeling and what I need.'
> 'You're a child - you respect your elders!'
> 'Teachers are supposed to treat all kids equally.'
> 'I don't care if we're not married. No cheating!'

Hanging on to unrealistic expectations does not help us resolve conflict effectively.

For example, suppose you expect that a good person will always do good and live up to your standards. The hard truth is that the finest of men and women might disappoint you. If the disappointment leads to a loss of respect and trust, it is wise to examine how this can damage your ability to work through a conflict.

Allow others to be human. Give grace and mercy. Forgive. Don't expect the impossible by putting people on a pedestal. No sane person can tolerate the pressure of being worshipped.

Identify your unrealistic expectations. Make a conscious decision to give them up, to accept reality, and set the stage for effective conflict resolution. In place of your unrealistic expectations, create new ones based on evidence from the past and what is happening in the present. If you have ongoing difficulty letting go of unrealistic expectations, it may be wise to seek professional help.

It's Not Personal

"Let us be kind to one another, for most of us are fighting a hard battle."
Rev. John Watson

A loving mother bought two expensive sweaters for her son to honor his twenty-first birthday. Getting ready for Sunday lunch, he wondered which sweater to wear. He chose one, admiring it in the mirror, knowing it would make his mom happy. As he walked into the dining room, Mom looked at him and said, "Oh! You don't like the other one?"

Every couple I've worked with can understand this. He says or does something, she takes it personally. She assumes he is trying to hurt her or that she's done something wrong. In some cases this might be true.

Bobbie and Clyde are struggling. In Bobbie's early years she endured the trauma of abandonment, sexual abuse and alcohol abuse. Not knowing that her trauma could be healed, she never sought help.

Now married to Clyde, the marriage in crisis, and they come for counseling. One of the major problems is that Bobbie's stress response is easily triggered; Clyde does not understand.

When Bobbie is triggered, Clyde holds her and hugs her - this is the last thing she wants. It scares her. Her body shakes and she says, "Let go!" He does so, but the feeling of rejection stays with him.

Having talked through this, however, he has come to realize it has nothing to do with him. This is her issue, and he might be wise to shift his belief about how to help her.

Nearly all of us have fallen into the "it's all about me" mentality. This is part of our flawed human nature. We have egos. The bigger our ego, the more readily we take things personally. The more we take things personally, the more intense our emotional reaction. And by now you know that emotional flooding makes conflict resolution impossible.

Setting the ego aside is a life-long challenge. When you're in conflict with someone, notice whether your ego is high gear. In that case, are you willing to change that? If you are, be assured, it's possible. But don't expect it to be easy. It's going to take the courage to put down your sword and shield and be yourself, just as you are.

How is this accomplished? You might consider the notion that you are not the center of the universe, you are not the judge of others, and that you do not have all the answers. That alone would be a good start.

Being Right

"Marriage has no guarantees. If that's what you're looking for, go live with a car battery."
Erma Bombeck, American Humorist

Is a win-win result ever possible? Or, is conflict a zero-sum game: that is, if one wins, the other must lose? In working through conflicts, do you always have to be right and to win? Does the other person have to be wrong and lose?

One of my clients tells me that his wife can be hard to talk to because she always has to have the last word. Even so, she's still not happy. Is it because when she wins (in her opinion), her husband's loss leaves him resentful? Thus, while she might relish the victory, she might realize that it's the relationship that really loses.

Maybe being right doesn't always make a person happy. And if you had to choose between being right and being happy, which would you choose?

Here's a tip from a wise old colleague of mine. When he and his wife disagree, he sometimes says, "You could be right." This soft, humble statement nourishes the relationship; to him the health of the relationship is more important than his need to be right.

Which one matters to you? Is it your ego and the need to win? Or, is it the quality of your relationship? If the relationship is what matters most, are you strong enough to let go of your ego and the need to win? Are you big enough to acknowledge that someone else is right? And that you could be wrong?

The Beauty of Going 'One Down'

"God opposes the proud, but gives grace to the humble." - James 4: 6

An inflated ego can block conflict resolution. To clarify, in this case ego refers to the need to be on top or the center of attention. A person with a big ego never willingly gives an inch.

You may agree that a humble attitude facilitates conflict resolution. But for some people humility does not come easily. Maybe the obstacle consists in the belief that being humble makes you feel small or less important than the other person. In that case, it's a worry. A worry is a kind of anxiety. And anxiety is a kind of fear.

You may also know that fear underlies many, if not all, destructive emotions. However, the big ego might readily say, 'I ain't scared of nobody or nothin'.'

When you think of humility as it relates to you, what comes to mind? Weakness? Letting others take advantage of you? Losing? Are you reluctant to take that position when you're in conflict with someone?

If you have a vintage channel available to your television service, look for the 1970's murder mystery series, "Columbo". Brilliantly played by Peter Falk, in every episode police Lt. Columbo uncovers the murderer by going 'one down' in relation to the prime suspect. He makes no attempt to dominate or intimidate. Instead, his respectful, self-controlled demeanor confuses and frustrates the suspect until eventually the means of the murder are exposed and the villain is caught.

Watching a television show may not change your life, but it can give you an idea of just one little thing you could do differently when trying to handle a conflict.

Letting Go

"Forgiveness is the fragrance that the violet sheds on the heel that has crushed it."
Mark Twain

"There is only one way to happiness and that is to cease worrying about things which are beyond the power of our will. " — Epictetus, Greek philosopher

All people experience suffering. All have been disappointed, betrayed or injured. After the damage has been done, letting go of the pain can be quite a challenge. The purpose of addressing this is that the failure to let go is a major obstacle to effective resolution of conflict.

Consider a few factors that keep us from letting go.

> We try to control things we can't control. Frustration follows.
> We demand that our ideal conditions be satisfied and deny what's really
>   happening.
> We can't get past the injustice of what has happened to us.
> We misunderstand how forgiveness should work.
> We associate with negative-minded people.
> Our mind works against us.
> > - It races.
> > - It loses focus.
> > - It worries about the future.
> > - It obsesses about the past.
> > - We believe we're out of options.
> > - We beat ourselves up with feelings of shame, guilt and failure.
> > - We use self-defeating words: "I can't!" "It's so hard." "I hate my life." "This
> >   is just the way I am." "I'm stuck."

Being unable or unwilling to let go is rooted in fear. For example, we refuse to forgive, because if we do so, we risk being hurt again. If we surround ourselves with people who support and reinforce our fears and our anger, letting go becomes nearly impossible.

What's to be done?

Avoid people who spread negativity. Focus on what we do have, instead of concentrating on what we're missing. Learn to distinguish what we can control, and what we cannot. Seek opportunities to make a positive difference in the lives of others. Learn the true purpose of forgiveness and how it works.

So many of us operate on "auto-pilot", trapped by self-defeating thoughts and beliefs, unaware that we can choose what to pay attention to and how to use our minds. Explore strategies to help you reprogram your mind to change your thinking, your habits and your choices.

Ask yourself, if you were to let go, what would it cost you? What is the fear associated with letting go? Is the fear justified? Or is this a product of your imagination?

Tapping into a reliable source of spiritual comfort would be a great thing to do. I recommend *The Serenity Prayer*.

"God, grant me the serenity
To accept the things I cannot change,
Courage to change the things I can, and
Wisdom to know the difference.

Living one day at a time,
Enjoying one moment at a time,
Accepting hardship as the pathway to peace.
Taking, as He did, this sinful world as it is,
Not as I would have it.
Trusting that He will make all things right
if I surrender to His will.
That I may be reasonably happy in this life,
And supremely happy with Him forever in the next.
Amen."

Defensiveness

"When we begin to build walls of prejudice, hatred, pride, and self-indulgence around ourselves, we are more surely imprisoned than any prisoner behind concrete walls and iron bars."
Mother Angelica

Once upon a time when we were young and helpless, we built walls for protection. Our walls kept us safe, so we came to rely on them. We fortified them, used them as protection in many situations and extended them well into later life, long after we no longer needed them.

Then one day we realized we weren't being invited to parties, included in games and sports, nor chosen as a partner in class projects. It even seemed like some of the kids were frightened of us. Did they hate us? Why? We never hurt anyone.

And when we grew up, the walls did some other bad things. They kept us feeling afraid and prevented us from reaching career goals and enjoying close relationships.

Walls offer protection, yes. But they also say, 'Stay out. Keep your distance.' If this is your general way with people, could it be an obstacle to conflict resolution?

Let's never forget that we are social beings. The reasonable person dislikes long-term separation from others. The wise person does not generally see others as the enemy.

If your habit of defensiveness is stealing your happiness, what are you going to do about it? Simply telling yourself to stop being defensive won't motivate you to change.

To change the defensiveness habit, ask yourself what the long-ago walls were meant to accomplish. What emotional need were the walls trying to meet? For example if anger is your problem, ask what purpose the anger originally served. You might realize that it was an expression of outrage about your hard life. You might notice that it's based in fear. The anger might have been a cry for sympathy or help. And for some reason, you've held on to it all your life.

Once you've identified the original purpose of the behavior, you can choose a new and healthy way to satisfy the emotional need. How to do that? Review the earlier section on Goal Setting, and notice the tips at the end of the Avoidance article, which follows immediately.

Avoidance

One night, as I walked home down a dark street, I saw a man near a corner up ahead. He was underneath a bright street lamp, looking down and pacing back and forth.

I stopped and asked if he needed help. He said that he'd dropped his keys.
I asked him where this happened.
Pointing down the block, he said, "Back there."
"Why are you looking for your keys over here?", I asked.
He answered, "There's no street light over there."

Since reasonable people don't enjoy rough personal conflict, they tend to avoid it when possible. This is not always a mistake. It's wise to pick our battles carefully.

I mention "rough personal conflict" in contrast to respectful, mature disagreements. A civil discussion of opposing views does not necessarily constitute a conflict.. You agree to disagree, and the relationship is unharmed. This is based on reason and common sense.

However, in person-to-person conflicts, common sense and reason often fly out the window. At those times it can be hard to tell whether the conflict should be addressed or avoided.

Habitual conflict avoidance predicts relationship failure. If you're a regular avoider, examine what you think, do and say when a conflict erupts. Do you tend to think …

> This is going to be bad
> I'm in trouble
> Something is wrong with me
> Something is wrong with the other person
> Something is wrong with our relationship
> He hates me
> I'm about to lose something big
> I'd better keep quiet
> I can't win, anyway

Notice that all of these assumptions are based on one emotion: fear. Now, you may notice a theme throughout this book.

Habitual avoidance produces bad feelings in both parties, and like a pressure cooker without a release valve, those emotions eventually explode.

Habitual conflict avoidance is not based on reason; it's based on anxiety, which is a form of fear. As we have all experienced, fear clouds our thinking. In the worst cases, one feels confused and agitated. The mind goes blank. The body gets tense, creating more anxiety and even panic. This prompts even more avoidance. The pattern has become set.

Fear of conflict intensifies when we doubt our judgment, can't express ourselves, we see no good options, and conclude that we can't cope.

it is important for people who habitually avoid conflict to learn self-expression and communication skills, and to consider ways to reprogram their belief systems so that they accept what they're feeling (review the chapter on Lying and See Yourself without Judging) and are brave enough to voice their emotions. Once these skills are in place, the avoidance habit can become a thing of the past.

The keys to entering the beautiful realm of self-assurance have everything to do with reprogramming negative thoughts and beliefs. If you are ready to get started on that, you have options. Reliable licensed therapists who practice clinical hypnosis, and who can teach you self-hypnosis. Self-affirming audio recordings. Therapies like Eye Movement Desensitization and Reprocessing (EMDR) are proven effective in this area, and so is meditation. I encourage you to do your own research and reach out. Help is available.

Attitude and Flexibility

"If you don't like something, change it. If you can't change it, change your attitude."
Maya Angelou

Successful negotiation occurs when neither party is completely happy, but both are satisfied. A positive attitude and the willingness to give a little aids in finding compromise.

The word "attitude" is interesting, especially with today's younger generation using the word to denote a bad attitude. As in, "Don't gimme no attitude."

But attitude is not just one thing. It's the totality of your physical emotional and mental states. The action of your mind: obsessing, racing, blank, muddled, or calm - your thoughts, your core beliefs about right and wrong, your tendency to judge others and your expectations about how conflict might work out.

When you address a conflict, check your attitude: positive or negative. Could your expectations, 'rules', emotions and ego ruin the party? Ask yourself what you need. What does the other party need and what is (s)he feeling? What are you willing to give? How do you expect your spouse, partner or child to behave? How do you expect this to work out?

Base your expectations not on the way things 'should' be (review the chapter on Unrealistic Expectations) but on your knowledge of the other person's past behavior and knowledge of yourself. Ideals are important. There is a place for idealism in this life. I argue that, in the resolution of conflict, the realistic, practical approach works better than the idealistic approach.

Now, to the question of flexibility. It is essential. In the first place, when conflict starts, emotions rise up and chaos can take over. People may say and do things you don't expect. You're taken by surprise and you might react badly. Communication breaks down, and you're done. In the second place, accept the fact that you can't have it all. When you accept that, you adapt. You take what you can get, and you don't fuss when you have to give something up.

Will it be easy to make the necessary changes? It depends on your attitude and motivation. And it may depend on whether you have to win or to be proved right.

Breaking the Pattern

"Everything can be taken from a man but one thing: the last of human freedoms - to choose one's attitude in any given set of circumstances, to choose one's own way."
Viktor Frankl, M.D., psychiatrist and Holocaust survivor

The resolution of some conflicts may not be as hard as it appears.

I once worked with a couple who were in daily conflict with each other. They were stuck in a number of unhealthy patterns. Among them were mutual blame, name-calling and resentment.

One pattern was that, not long after the birth of their daughter, they rarely spent time together as a couple. Their conflict intensified, their anger at one another increased, and eventually they each preferred being with their child rather than with each other.

It seemed a good idea to take a directive approach with these good people - to give them a firm, gentle nudge in a new direction, encouraging them to do just one thing differently. As a result, he agreed to make one small change in his behavior. That is, he agreed to go on a date with his wife, and go to the restaurant she suggested, instead of dismissing her as he usually did. She agreed to go on outings with him and the baby, even on days when she said she needed 'alone time.'

Making little changes such as these could be enough to remind the other of the importance of giving a little, now and then.

In certain cases, when you want to address personal conflicts, all that's necessary is to break up the pattern. Do one thing differently from the way you usually do, and see what happens.

Looking Good

"Do nothing out of selfish ambition or vain conceit. Rather, in humility value others above yourselves, not looking to your own interests but each of you to the interests of the others."
Philippians 2: 3-4

Since anger fuels conflict, we might wonder what fuels anger. The answer? Lots of things. In this case, let's look at the mother of all fuels: humiliation. For some, it's the most sensitive of all triggers.

Working with teens at a residential treatment facility, my staff and I learned to address a kid when he or she was out of line. One cardinal rule: Never encounter the teen in front of other kids. Separate him or her from the others, and only then point out the bad behavior and explain the consequences.

There's a real human reason that no one wants to look bad. Looking bad means rejection, criticism, contempt and maybe even being kicked out of the group. The ultimate fear involved in all this? It's the fear of being alone.

This applies not only to youth, but to everyone. If you have conflict with someone, and one or both of you tends to air it in front of others … don't! Now, you may be tempted to do it, because the other person did it. Do you really want to get into that childish "he hit me first" kindergarten stuff?

Failing to Prepare

"If you fail to plan for success, you are planning for failure."

Adequate preparation is a great aid to conflict management. Athletes and musicians warm up before playing. Smart job-seekers research the company before an interview. Expert negotiators, lawyers and politicians never enter a big meeting unprepared.

A young couple, married less than a year, came for counseling. In the first session - which turned out to be the last - I sensed that they hardly knew each other. They had dated in college, and, after a while, decided it was time to meet the parents. Following the first meeting with her folks, her mom told her daughter to marry him. So they married. And it was not easy.

As we talked, noting their lack of connection, I asked how well they knew one another. I asked whether they'd ever talked about this thing called love. Blank stares. To jump-start the conversation, I offered some ideas, such as … some say love is a feeling … others say love is a verb, it's about what you do for another person … love is commitment ... love is sacrifice, hard work, etc. She said immediately that love is an emotion. He said, just as firmly, love is about action. The confused look they shared with one another said it all.

Lack of preparation can play out in very troubling ways. I've treated married couples who never talked about having children before the wedding day. Here's what I heard in one case.

She: "I just assumed you wanted kids. Everyone wants kids!"
He: "What do you mean, everyone wants kids? I never wanted to be a dad."
She: "I can't believe this. What's the point of getting married if you don't want kids?!"
He: "What's the point of anything? I married you because I love you. That's all. No kids!"

Amazing, isn't it?

Some ministers will perform a marriage ceremony only if the couple attends pre-marital counseling. This may seem demanding or judgmental. But think about it. The minister prefers to know that both members of the couple have the insight to prepare for life's challenges; that is, to find their points of agreement and disagreement before getting married.

When you attempt to work out a conflict, do you dive in without thinking? Do you start arguing before you're fully informed? If so, you will benefit by agreeing to never again do such a thing.

When addressing a conflict, be wise. Think about it in advance. Imagine how the other person will react if you do this or that. Imagine how your attitude and actions could set the stage for a positive outcome. And remember this: the conflict resolution process will probably end the same way it started.

The Last Straw - A Sad Story

"Never cry just because someone hurt you.
Just smile and thank God for having the chance to find someone better."

Robin, 40 years of age and the father of a 16-year-old, Rick, sought help because his wife, Marian, was planning to divorce him.

This didn't come out of the blue. It was preceded by years of hurtful and discouraging events. Along the way he'd experienced deep depression. During those dark days, for months at a time, Robin would suffer in silence, hide in the bedroom or rail in anger at his wife and son. This went on through much of Rick's childhood.

Then came the last straw. He wanted to buy a motorcycle.

Some months prior, Marian had witnessed a fatal motorcycle accident in which the cyclist crashed into the side of a semi trailer. Although she was able to drive away quickly and didn't see the aftermath, the memory stayed with her. She begged him not to go ahead, but he dismissed her fears and bought the motorcycle.

After all the negativity and rejection she'd felt for so many years, she couldn't take any more.

You've read about the importance of respect, listening and validation. Breaking just one conflict resolution principle is bad enough. Breaking several at the same time multiplies the damage.

Robin didn't listen to Marian, he disrespected her wishes and he invalidated her fears. All these added up to a blatant disregard for her happiness. Clueless that her staying in the marriage was a miracle in itself, he was shocked when she said she was leaving.

Manipulation

"And Jesus said to his disciples, 'Temptations to sin are sure to come; but woe to him by whom they come! It would be better for him if a millstone were hung round his neck and he were cast into the sea, than that he should cause one of these little ones to sin.'" - Luke 17: 1-2

There's a classic comic film entitled, *You Can't Cheat An Honest Man*. This is an old saying, and in many ways it's true. Con artists succeed by making their victims feel extra special or by convincing them they're getting a deal - something for nothing, or something no one else is getting.

Con artists exploit your appetites and your emotions in order to control you and use you. If you don't want something for nothing, and if you don't allow your emotions to control you, the con artist fails.

How does the manipulator use our emotions against us? Think of the Seven Deadly Sins: Sloth (laziness), Pride, Anger, Greed, Gluttony, Lust, Envy. When we are governed by the emotions connected to these and other character flaws, we are in a weakened state. And while we are in that state, the manipulator can control us.

People most vulnerable to manipulation are those who feel emotionally needy. It may go back to childhood. Something was missing - the love, respect and protection of a parent, for example - and has left one feeling a void. Such people yearn strongly for acceptance and approval. and they believe another person can provide it. This is highly questionable. Even the most caring person can't replace a parent.

One particularly devastating kind of neediness is the need to be needed. For example, the woman who is regularly abused by her boyfriend stays with him because, as she might say, "I love him. He needs me. He's had such a rough life. He doesn't really mean those things he does. No one understands him, except for me. I'm all he's got." You see how a manipulator could use that to his advantage.

When you've had conflict with someone, did you ever wonder if the other person was tricking or deceiving you - trying to convince you that you are wrong, crazy or stupid?

When kids do this, we give consequences - that's pretty simple. But when adults do it, especially when the manipulator is a family member, it can get complicated. Please keep the following idea in mind.

In most cases a manipulator cannot harm you, unless you allow it.

Allow it? Why would anyone allow himself to be manipulated? Is it a conscious decision, or does it just happen? The question has no ready answers. Each situation is unique, and, even if the 'victim' chooses to be manipulated, that choice generally is a result of subconscious processes.

Rather than focusing on the cause, let's see what can be done about it. To avoid being manipulated, we must recognize the manipulative behavior as soon as possible. This only happens when we are thinking clearly. See my article on *Lies, Tricks and Other Deceptions* in Part 3.

The moment you spot the manipulation, do not speak or react in any way, Slow down your response time, take a deep breath, think about what's happening and what the other person is doing. Use the skills in Part 1, especially the 5-Second Rule.

Once we know what the manipulator is doing, we have a choice: to respond or not to respond. And if we respond, how should we respond and for what purpose?

Another principle to remember:

> ***A manipulator cannot harm you if you don't need or want anything from him/her.***

Avoiding the clutches of a manipulator calls on us to be honest about what we're experiencing, and honest enough to admit whether we're avoiding taking responsibility for our well-being.

If this sounds scary, be reassured that many people who've suffered in at the hands of a manipulator have found peace. Such peace, however, is not to be found in the realms of this material world. Anyone who struggles with painful feelings and who has been repeatedly manipulated can look to a true source of wisdom and healing. I say the source is a relationship with God. You are free to say it in your own way.

Regardless of one's belief system, one must never look to a living person for emotional rescue. This merely repeats the habit of dependency and keeps one vulnerable to further manipulation.

Roadblocks

"If something can go wrong, it will go wrong." - Murphy's Law

A hypothetical couple, Meryl and Dustin argue daily, about everything. Money, the kids, family relations. Their roadblocks may look something like the following, which is just a partial list.

1. Dustin wants to address conflicts immediately. Meryl can't talk about them right then; she needs time to think. Dustin is impatient and relentless. He follows her around the house, not letting her off the hook. She yells, "Leave me alone!" He says, "Fine!", dashes to the car and roars away into the night.

2. To Dustin the problem is urgent; not so for Meryl.

3. Dustin works twelve-hour days, waking up at 4:30 a.m. He needs to be in bed by 8:30. And wouldn't you know it? That's just when Meryl wants to talk. Bad timing is always a major obstacle.

4. Stubbornness. Refusal to yield. Insistence on being right and having the last word.

5. One or both parties refuse to express themselves honestly and directly.

6. One of them can overpower the other; emotionally and in other ways. An imbalance of powers inhibits conflict resolution.

If you can agree to a new set of rules for resolution, relief will come. (See *The Rules of Engagement Questionnaire* in Part 3). For example, if you interrupt one another, agree on this deal: each time you interrupt, you put a dollar in a jar with your name on it. Let's say you've interrupted ten times and put in ten dollars; you must use that money to do something nice for the other person. In this way, you can motivate each other to change the habits that create roadblocks.

Use this approach, and you will grasp a new and precious understanding:

The subject matter of the conflict is rarely the real problem.
The real problem is the way you relate to one another.

If you're unable to resolve relationship conflicts, don't address the conflict itself. Instead, invite the other person to talk calmly about the roadblocks. Start to identify them. Then, one after the other, explore ways to eliminate them.

Carrot vs. Stick

*"Change will happen when the pain of the present moment
outweighs the fear of changing."* - A common axiom for psychotherapists

Improving your conflict resolution skills requires changes in your beliefs, thinking and behaviors. You can turbo-charge your progress by understanding what motivates you to do hard things, like changing a behavior or thought pattern.

Consider your childhood. All kids misbehave. Some parents handle it well, others do not. If your parents raised you right, that success depended partly on her understanding of you and how she might motivate you to correct a bad behavior.

Now, what about you? How did you decide to behave properly? Was it the fear of punishment, the fear of disappointing your parents or the fear of losing privileges? Or was it the hope that, if you were good, you'd be rewarded? That is, are you motivated to change by the fear of losing something that matters to you, or by the hope of gaining something you'd love to have?

If the pain of mishandling conflict has gotten to you, and you still resist change, you could be holding on to something you're not willing to give up. This 'something' maintains the resistance to change. Almost certainly, fear or anxiety is driving this resistance.

Perhaps you have not yet realized that the fear of change is rooted in mistaken assumptions. For example, maybe you don't believe change is possible. Or you can't imagine the glorious possibilities that could open up, once you let go of the fear.

If you're considering professional help to get 'un-stuck', consider this: what you're experiencing is taking place unconsciously. You're not shooting yourself in the foot on purpose. Thus, therapy that helps to uncover unconscious resources - hypnosis and EMDR, for example - may be indicated. Talk therapy may help somewhat, but for most people it may not be enough.

The Trouble with 'Why'

"True wisdom comes to each of us when we realize how little we understand about life, ourselves, and the world around us." - Socrates

Years ago, I counseled a fifteen year-old boy, Skip. His parents, Roy and Dale, placed him at our residential treatment center because of his depression, defiance and poor school work. A few months after Skip arrived, he did something that angered his parents. He made choices that ruined their plans to bring him home for Christmas.

In a family therapy session, Roy said to Skip, "I just want to know why you did that. That's all I want!"

No answer.

"Skip! Just tell me why!!"

The boy looked down, shook his head slowly, and said quietly, "I don't know."

Roy wanted Skip to know that, if he could understand Skip's reasons, he would not be angry. Unfortunately, Skip heard Roy's questioning as a challenge he could not meet.

Roy erupted, "What do you mean you don't know!? You messed up! Your sister was bawling when we left Akron this morning. What's wrong with you?!"

Skip's head dropped onto his hands, and he started crying. Dale and Roy shared a look of utter exasperation.

There are at least two problems with demanding to know why. Bad choices are usually impulsive choices. The offender can't explain them, because his actions were not deliberate. But demanding to know why assumes that the offender 'should' have an honest answer. If he doesn't, he's lying, stubborn, disrespectful or stupid. Secondly, the offender is forced to admit ignorance. Skip felt stupid and ashamed, and concluded,'I'm just no good.' or 'Something is wrong with me.'

Instead of asking why, ask 'what'? Roy might have said to Skip, "Skip, son, what was going on when you stopped doing your chores and stopped handing in your homework? Can you help me understand what was getting in the way of you doing the right thing? If you can let me know, maybe we could figure this out together."

To be clear, it's not always wrong to ask why. If you must do so, ask the question with a curious approach and with caring and compassion, taking care that your tone does not put the other person on the defensive.

See Yourself without Judging

"Do not seek revenge or bear a grudge against anyone among your people, but love your neighbor as yourself. I am the Lord." - Leviticus 19: 18

The Judaeo-Christian Scriptures teach us to love others as we love ourselves. In this sense, as many Bible scholars have long agreed, loving ourselves means caring for and respecting ourselves. We're not meant to judge ourselves - or others - harshly. We might, at times, judge the wisdom of our actions, but that is completely different from judging our value as human beings.

Wisdom tells us to correct our errors in a calm and reasonable manner. However, many of us do the opposite. We mess up, get angry, criticize ourselves, and give ourselves negative messages.

Self-condemnation prevents us from seeing ourselves accurately, it negates our positive qualities, and it creates mental agitation and confusion. As you know by now, the agitated mind is not capable of effective conflict resolution.

If you had to grade yourself on honesty - honesty with yourself and your willingness and ability to admit your errors and your flaws - what grade would you give yourself? Are you willing and able to look inside your heart and mind without judging yourself? Are you able to let go of anger and disappointment in yourself?

If you tend to beat yourself up, you may benefit from mindfulness meditation. The information about this practice is readily available in books, online articles possibly even from one of your doctors. See the Recommended Reading list at the back of the book. Some of the great benefits of mindfulness meditation:

> It slows down an overactive mind
> It reminds you to stay focused on the present moment
> It trains you to see yourself and others without judging
> It promotes relaxation and freedom from worry
> It cultivates wisdom

If you are not comfortable sitting in silence for 10 to 20 minutes, try five minutes. One minutes. As you read in Part 1, you may prefer a moving meditation.

Trust Your Gut

"Things are not always as they appear to be.
People are not always who they appear to be."

In some conflict situations, reason disagrees with emotions, resulting in internal conflict and confusion. We question our judgment, and misunderstand other people's speech, behavior and motives. Thus, bad decisions follow.

The confusion may be due to low self-confidence and/or the lack of problem-solving and decision-making skills. Or it may be the result of outside manipulation from individuals and institutions, such as companies, religious groups, and the government.

Lying is perhaps the most common manipulation. Some folks are better liars than others. Some people know how to spot a liar. Others are clueless. But even a skilled reader of body language can be fooled.

By studying nonverbal communication, you can learn the tell-tale signs of dishonesty. This skill would serve you well throughout your life. Interestingly, though, you might also find that in some situations you're better off relying on your gut feeling.

If you're more logical than emotional, you may not trust a gut feeling. But consider this. Many of life's biggest decisions have nothing to do with reasoning. Do people fall in love based on logic? Does logic determine voting choices? Does the stock market tick up or down based on reasoning? Not even close. All of these decisions are driven by emotion.

The fact is that hunches and feelings can play a larger role in our lives than we may admit. If you learn to trust your feelings, your intuition, your awareness of yourself, you might expand your ability to prevent conflict from arising.

You can get started by taking an honest look at yourself. Do you lack self-confidence? Do you doubt your talents, your intelligence and your ability to understand people? Are you limiting your personal growth by negative beliefs? If so, you will benefit from professional help to recondition your thinking and your beliefs about who you are and what you're capable of. Chances are good that you have far more to offer than you ever dreamed of.

Abuse & Fear

"I learned that courage was not the absence of fear, but the triumph over it. The brave man is not he who does not feel afraid, but he who conquers that fear." - Nelson Mandela

Victims of sexual, physical and emotional abuse are the greatest source of insight into the after-effects of these various forms of abuse. One of the most common after-effects is the difficulty in handling conflict.

Often, people who are in a relationship with an abuse/trauma survivor fail to understand why she 'overreacts' when she's stressed. They don't understand trauma triggers, and can not see that a trauma survivor's life can be plagued by fear and anxiety. A person whose day-to-day life is easily disrupted by fear and anxiety is likely to be mistrustful in general, to avoid closeness, to be afraid of change and risk, to feel depressed, angry and to suffer from mood swings.

The spouse, partner, friend or relative of an abuse/trauma survivor feels frustrated, confused, and, not knowing how to respond properly, he may criticize the survivor's 'crazy' behavior. This is a major obstacle to effective conflict resolution.

If you are an abuse/trauma survivor, yourself, do you know how your trauma experience has damaged your ability to handle conflict? Remember that fear is the driving emotion in those cases. If you wish resolution of the trauma, the fear must be addressed. You may doubt that this is possible, but I assure you, countless people have succeeded in overcoming trauma-based fears.

Fortunately, many roads lead to freedom from fear. Developing expertise in an activity you love: the arts, sports, business, helping people. Therapy, meditation and martial arts can help too. When you begin to look around, you'll see that you have options. And this realization alone could put you right on the path to freedom from fear.

If you're ready to seek freedom from fear, ask yourself whether you truly believe you can be free of fear. Are you willing to try? Will it be worth it?

As you may have read here, Scripture tells us that anxiety - fear of what might happen - does not co-exist with gratitude. The mind cannot be grateful and anxious at the same time. If you cultivate the habit of gratitude, you will notice that anxiety tends to subside.

Every day, give thanks for at least three things that went well that day. It works very nicely to do so as you're drifting off to sleep. Make this a nightly habit and see what good things can develop.

The Impact of Trauma

"I told my mother at about the seventh year of therapy that I had been abused sexually by my father, and she hung up the phone on me." - Anne Heche, actress

It's well known that psychological trauma hampers the ability to resolve conflict.

Psychological trauma is not just one thing. It can be a single event or a series of events which leaves the victim in a prolonged state of distress. The distress includes the following, all of which can block the ability to function effectively:

Painful emotions
Frightening memories
Disturbing and intrusive thoughts
Distorted beliefs
Self-defeating habits
Automatic physical reactions
An ongoing sense of dread and instant arousal
Extreme watchfulness for signs of danger
Nightmares
Flashbacks
Toxic relationships
Anxiety and depression
Irrational anger
Losing awareness of the here and now
Apathy and emotional numbing
Physical symptoms and health problems
Extreme measures to avoid being reminded (drugs, alcohol)

A young woman comes for therapy. Her stated problem is that she becomes upset for no reason. She can't express her feelings. Her husband does not understand. She appears angry and afraid. He feels helpless and confused. She becomes more upset, and the conflict escalates. The future of this relationship looks dim.

Psychological trauma changes how the brain works. The brain of a traumatized person slips quickly into the state called, "fight-flight-freeze." The spouse must understand this and must exercise patience with the unique problem the survivor is grappling with. Review that section in Part 1. Because she cannot regulate her emotions, she can't always calm down. When stress rises up, her awareness is thrust back in time, and she loses touch with the here and now. She needs healing. The spouse needs education.

When in the grip of a stress reaction, resolution of conflict is impossible. Even worse news: if the victim is not getting help, the health risks are massive. Emotional stress can impact nearly every system in the body, as well as the immune system. In other words, poorly managed stress can literally make you sick.

But don't despair. Healing is possible, and the paths to healing are numerous. If you or your partner, child or spouse is a trauma survivor, they need to know that help is available, even for people who've experienced the worst imaginable horrors. Do not hesitate to consult a professional, whether you or the other person is the trauma survivor.

You can find a trauma specialist in your area by contacting the International Society for the Study of Trauma and Dissociation (ISST-D) by going to: www.isst-d.org.

The No-Win Conflict

"Never mud wrestle with a pig. You just get dirty and the pig enjoys it."

Call it stubbornness, persistence, lack of perspective or just plain stupidity. We've all done it. Being stuck in an unresolved conflict, and refusing to accept that no solution exists, or that we lack the ability or the intelligence to sort it out. We tell ourselves, "I'm no quitter, I'm not giving up."

Generally speaking, we admire the no-quit personality. If their goals are noble, we call them heroes. Think of George Washington, Helen Keller, Martin Luther King, Jr., Thomas Edison, Rosa Parks and Winston Churchill. Without them our world would be a less happy place.

However - and this is a big however - in some cases the no-quit attitude can create problems rather than solving them. This is true when the no-quitter meets a conflict that has no solution. In old fashioned terms, "when an immovable object meets an irresistible force."

Insoluble conflicts have existed forever. Wars, the battle between the sexes, the struggle between good and evil. On a global scale, grand ideas aimed at addressing impossible problems have been presented by smart, well-meaning people. All have failed.

Such problems exist on a personal scale, too. You might know someone who will never change or a situation that could change, but over which you have no influence.

What do we do with this? We can accept this reality, and we can learn to tell the difference between a conflict that we can change, as opposed to one that we cannot. (Remember the Serenity Prayer). We can realize whether we are applying a death-grip to the need for control. And we can make a commitment to ourselves to learn the life lesson of acceptance and discernment. You may want to re-read the sections on *Refusing to Accept Reality* and *Letting Go*.

Prevention

"We live in a country that used to have a can-do attitude, and now we have a 'what-can-you-do-for-me?' attitude, and what I try to do is find ways that we can develop common ground."
Ben Carson, M.D., Pediatric Neurosurgeon

Group-against-group conflicts have existed throughout history. They are impressed into our world, as a colorfast dye becomes a permanent part of a fabric. Some have been resolved, but, as already mentioned, other conflicts appear permanent.

One vivid example is the Israeli-Palestinian conflict. Decade after decade, many of the smartest and most powerful world leaders have failed to bring it to full resolution.

Back in the 1980's a celebrated international lawyer named Samuel Pisar proposed the idea that such conflicts are less likely to occur when the parties - nations, corporations, etc. - do business with each other. In fact the validity of that idea has held up, according to accounts of real people from the Holy Land. Those witnesses are Israelis and Palestinians who lived together for many years, side by side, in peace. Their kids went to school together. They cooperated as neighbors. And how did this work? It was because their livelihoods were closely intertwined. They did business with each other, and they came to trust and respect one another. The bottom line: they needed each other in order to make a living.

When your livelihood is on the line, it doesn't make sense to squabble. When you have developed a relationship that includes trust and respect based on common interests and goals, conflict is a distant thought.

You can apply this to the conflicts in your life. Establish common ground by finding a common interest between you and the other person. It may be related to work, recreation, or a spiritual or social mission. Once you have found something that's important to both of you, you both gain a sense of connection, common purpose and value, and you may find that your previous squabbles no longer matter.

Double Your Treasure

"The unexamined life is not worth living." - Socrates

At our first meeting, new clients are oriented to my two-track idea. In fact this book's approach mirrors what takes place in the therapy room.

Nearly everyone who comes for help says something like, "I don't know how to let go of my past or ... communicate with my wife ... handle my boss ... stop feeling guilty ... deal with my child ... etc. They tell me they need tools, skills, knowledge. This is what I call "Track 1. The Skill and Knowledge Track". Very important stuff. All about communication, problem-solving and conflict resolution.

But that's not the whole story. Heightened self-awareness and insight into our strengths and weaknesses is equally important. For example, understanding our self-defeating thoughts and habits: negativity, cynicism, judging ourselves and others, poor self-control, bitterness and resentment, etc. This is what happens in "Track 2. The Insight Track."

These two tracks work together. The more we practice effective communication and conflict resolution skills, the more we understand our limitations. The more we understand the price we pay for our limitations, the more we are motivated to improve our skills. This is a beautiful partnership.

Baggage

"And now, dear brothers and sisters, whatever is true, whatever is noble, whatever is right, whatever is pure, whatever is lovely, whatever is admirable — if anything is excellent or praiseworthy — think about such things." - Philippians 4: 8

Many people have been scarred by painful memories, which, even though they seem to have disappeared, can resurface when stress levels rise. As you've read in the trauma chapter, the impact of painful memories hampers effective conflict resolution.

We refer to these memories as "baggage" - the exhausting burden of unresolved personal issues. Baggage affects every aspect of our lives: our beliefs, our relationships, workplace interactions, spending habits … you name it.

Corky and Lorna, a middle-aged couple, come for counseling. Lorna has three grown children from previous relationships. Corky has two. She seeks help, because she can not tolerate his angry outbursts. They have no idea where to begin, and it's no wonder. Their individual problems go way back in time. They are both carrying so much emotional baggage that conflict resolution has become impossible.

As a young girl, Lorna had been sexually molested by her father. After her parents divorced, her mother married a man who abused her physically and emotionally. She now says, "it's all behind me now, I don't think about it anymore". But clearly she has not recovered, because her reactions to her husband's anger fall towards two extremes: she freezes in terror or she lashes out. Corky, on the other hand, has not recovered from his ex-wife's infidelity. If Lorna looks at another man, he becomes suspicious and questions her. She reacts defensively, as if she's being attacked. You see what's happening.

Recall the idea that many, if not all, destructive emotions are fear-based. Ask yourself whether your baggage has anything to do with fear. Fear of losing something important - affection, security, respect or physical comfort. Ask yourself whether these fears were, at one time, legitimate. Ask yourself whether you have allowed your thinking and your emotions to be molded by painful experiences, so much so, that you continue to react to stresses in self-defeating ways.

If that is the case, be reassured that this condition can change, if you are motivated enough to do so. Please review *Carrot vs. Stick*.

Unloading your baggage, thus allowing yourself to handle conflict and stress, is not a one-and-done deal. It's a life-long, ongoing process, which requires daily practice.

Select one of your self-defeating habits, thoughts or beliefs. Actively and vigorously give yourself messages every day, which counteract that habit, thought or belief. Write yourself reminders and place them all around your home. Listen to inspiring words and music that help you to remember to drop the old baggage - and even more importantly - acquire a new set of luggage.

Avoid people who reinforce your tendency to hold on to the baggage. Be with people who have figured out how to let go of it, and learn from them.

Defeating the Bully

"Verbal judo is about transforming negative energy directed towards you so that the aggressor chooses to reconsider and refrain from hostility."

I once had the pleasure of working with a 12-year-old boy who was being bullied.

Call him Andy. Andy was in sixth grade at a school where I interned once a week. He was referred to me after getting repeated detentions due to talking rudely and apparently threatening another boy.

This is what Andy told me.

Nearly every day at school, an older boy taunted Andy and called him stupid. The bully was shrewd. He didn't raise his voice. Andy, on the other hand, would fire back in a loud voice, "Shut up, you're stupid!" Thus it went. It was Andy, never the bully, who got into trouble.

I asked Andy if he'd ever watched martial arts movies. He said yes. I demonstrated with one simple, harmless move (not being a martial artist, myself) how martial artists win by using the opponent's energy and momentum against him. They throw the opponent off balance.

"You know what I'm talking about, right?," I asked.

Andy said, "Uh-huh", with a knowing smile.

I suggested he could do this with words, too.

"Okay. The next time the bully calls you stupid, you might say, 'You know, I've been thinking, and you're right. I am kind of stupid. Can you help me be smart?' After all, I explained, we're all stupid - or just not competent - in some ability or another."

He nodded, smiled slyly and his eyes twinkled right up. Leaving our meeting, he thanked me and said he couldn't wait to try this.

Two weeks later, I asked Andy how it went. Once again came the sly smile.

He said, "I told him, 'You're right, I'm kind of stupid. Would you help me with my homework?'"

This made my day. I said, "How about that? And how's it going? Does he still bother you?"

"No, when I told him that, he looked at me like I was crazy, and now he leaves me alone."

Dependency

"Don't shop for food when you're hungry."

Emotional and financial dependency render a person powerless. The dependent person feels he can not or should not assert himself. When conflict arises, the outcome will be bad.

Two women, both in their thirties, having no relationship to one another, come for individual counseling. I'll call them Tiffany and Brittany. Each of them is in a bad marriage.

Tiffany has three children from a previous relationship, plus a toddler from her boyfriend, and is now pregnant by him. Her boyfriend is cheating. This is not his first infidelity. Tiffany hopes that couples counseling can help the situation.

Brittany has two children. She says her husband is verbally abusive and selfish. She is miserable. He calls her crazy. Lacking work skills, she is completely dependent on him. To make matters worse, he is well connected in his community. Brittany hopes that couples counseling will help.

Both women chose to rely on men without preparing themselves for independence. Both men took advantage, and why not? After all, as they might say, 'She can't leave. Where's she gonna go?' Not all men would act this way, but these two women seemed to attract the domineering type. This is explained further in at least one section in the article, *Lies, Tricks and Other Deceptions* in Part 3.

Brittany's and Tiffany's refusal to be self-reliant has trapped them; they have created their own victimhood. Unless something or someone intervenes, they will never be able to cope with conflict.

While all close adult relationships require mutually respectful interdependence - the two people need each other equally - such interdependence must be marked by respect, fairness and decency.

To sum up, we will be wise to acquire skills and knowledge about handling conflict and to create a lifestyle that promotes well-being and harmony. Additionally. we are wise to know how to prevent disaster from striking; for example, by not allowing ourselves to be taken advantage of by making ourselves powerless and dysfunctionally dependent upon others.

When Sharing Yourself, Be Wise

"He who goes about gossiping reveals secrets;
therefore do not associate with one who speaks foolishly." - Proverbs 20: 19

"A dishonest man spreads strife, and a whisperer separates close friends." - Proverbs 16:28

It's not healthy to keep our problems to ourselves. Most of us need to vent. Even so, when sharing our burdens, we can also exercise wisdom.

Conflicts are often aggravated in a particular way. One or both persons talk about it with people who are not involved.

Consider this common situation. A mom or dad is having a terrible time with one of the kids. The youngster has behaved badly at a family event. The parent feels the need to explain or apologize to a family member. The conversation goes on and the parent, who is now on a roll, reveals her child's other misdeeds. Whether the word gets around or not, if the child finds out that mom or dad is 'telling everyone', the child will be rightfully upset and may no longer trust mom or dad.

Only people who are party to a conflict should be involved in resolving it. In a family setting, if the conflict affects everyone, everyone should participate. If you choose to bring in a friend, family member, professional or mediator, everyone must agree to it.

The next time you have a problem with someone, the most effective and fairest way to go about fixing it is to be direct. Go to the person privately and try to work it out.

Resolving conflicts can seem hard, even almost impossible at times. And, as mentioned in a previous section, some conflicts may never find resolution. But conflicts are more likely to be resolved when everyone respects the confidentiality and privacy of everyone else.

PART 3

More Stuff

*"If you keep on doing what you've been doing,
you'll keep on getting what you've been getting."*

The following additional resources, when used consistently, will enhance your confidence and grow your wisdom as you continue to manage conflict effectively.

The first item is a detailed explanation of the "I" Statement. This is included, because most people tend to misuse it at first. The problem appears to be that the honest expression of emotion does not come naturally to most of us; when you first use this tool, it might feel artificial. However, this step-by-step explanation can help anyone use the "I" Statement effectively. If you keep practicing, you'll see how beautifully it works.

Also included are tools to help you anticipate problems, deal with difficult people, foster self-knowledge, break bad communication habits and build trust and understanding.

The "I" Statement Reloaded

When you use the "I" Statement, keep it brief. The following illustrations will help you do that.

Key Principles:
    Used correctly, the "I" Statement does not provoke defensiveness.
    It invites the other person to tell you whether or not he cares how you feel.

Sam and Julie are at it again. Follow along and see how they might get it right, or mess it up.

1) Julie expresses a feeling:

This is the right way to do it:
Julie: "Sam, when you _____ (fill in the blank with a NON-JUDGMENTAL word for the offensive behavior)… I feel _____(fill in the blank with a genuine FEELING/EMOTION word, not an opinion, evaluation or judgment)."

This can be misspoken in two ways:

a) misstating the first part by using a loaded word, like "When you accused me …." Don't put your spin on it. Just say the words Sam said or the things he did.

b) misstating the second part by saying, "I felt like you hate me" or "I felt like you wanted something from me.", or "You just want your way all the time."

Notice the two illustrations that follow:

Incorrect: "Sam, when you forgot about me and didn't call, I felt like you just didn't care." An error is made in both parts of this communication. First, "Sam, when you forgot about me (that's an opinion, which may not be true) …secondly, "you just didn't care" is an evaluation or judgment of Sam's feelings.

Correct: "Sam, when you didn't call last night, I felt hurt." You see? Simple and brief.

By doing this correctly, the other person can respond to your emotions without feeling the need to defend himself – you haven't accused or blamed him. Now, the burden is on him to give you feedback. He may choose one of two options: 1) He cares how you feel. Or 2) He doesn't care.

2) Sam's Response

Option #1: Sam cares about your feelings. He'll say something like, "I had no idea!" or, "I didn't know you felt like that. I'm sorry. I'll do better next time."

Option #2: Sam doesn't care how you feel. He might say, "What about the time you forgot _____? You're always doing that stuff to me. I'm sick and tired of you blaming me all the time." This is out of bounds. Neither person may bring in another issue when she makes the statement, or when she responds to the statement. Stay on one topic at a time.

3) Julie's Response if Sam doesn't care how she feels

Julie has two choices:

Option #1: Julie may re-state her feeling: "Maybe I didn't make myself clear. Let me try again. I was really hurt when you _____ _____. Do you care how I feel?"

Sam may understand and choose to make up.

Option #2: If Sam still doesn't care, then Julie may choose to set a limit. She has the right to protect herself from Sam's lack of caring. So, Julie may say, "Okay, you've got a right to your position. But I have rights, too, so I'm going to limit our contact." This will take various forms, depending on the relationship: workplace relationship, husband-wife, parent-child, neighbor-neighbor, etc. Say it in a way that fits your style.

If you use the "I" statement correctly, and the other person responds negatively or says you're out of line, get a 'reality check' from a trusted advisor, in order to validate your complaint.

"I" statements should be used to praise and to affirm others, as well. If you do all these things, you'll be managing conflict by means of prevention.

Practice the "I" statement regularly, so it feels natural. Make it part of the way you express yourself to those who matter to you, and it will pay off.

Building Bridges of Trust

"In all relationships, we are always building one of two things: bridges or walls."

Poorly managed conflict can break trust. This item will help you understand how to regain it. The word, "friend" refers to anyone with whom we wish to develop trust.

Teamwork – Joint activities – household chores, special projects and volunteer efforts, for example – are great for developing cooperation, compromise and unity all of which strengthen the bond of trust.

Talk – Talk to your friend about the things that matter. Respect his concerns and preferences.

Listen – Listening closely encourages the other person to let down her guard.

Kindness and Gentleness – A key to establishing a sense of emotional safety, our first non-physical need.

Self-control – When we appropriately process our stresses, others feel safe with us. Acknowledge your bad habits and impulsive behavior. Think, before acting or speaking.

Praise – Help your friend build self-worth by affirming her sincere efforts, whether she succeeds or not.

Recreation – Have fun together. Enjoy friendly competition. If you lose, do so graciously.

Sharing – Share your knowledge, experience and wisdom. It's a blessing to them and you.

Tenacity - Never give up. If you drive forward through frustration, you can be trusted with tough tasks.

Gratitude – We all need a little appreciation and gratitude. Don't be stingy with it. Give it freely.

Forgiveness – Anyone who holds grudges makes it harder for others to trust him.

Empathy – Trying to sense other people's feelings makes them more likely to trust you.

Loyalty – You can be trusted when you don't turn your back on your friend.

Mutual Self Exposure/Vulnerability – Show your true self with no fear of judgment or rejection. It encourages others to be open, as well. When you are free to be yourselves, closeness and trust will abound.

Patience - Impatience is a sign of immaturity. Would you trust an adult who acts immaturely?

Humility - Do you trust someone who is easily offended and takes things personally? Or … are you more likely to trust someone who accepts criticism without getting upset?

Courage - A person who allows fear to control him cannot be trusted.

Ask for advice - This elevates the other person. Thus, putting them at ease and building trust.

Respect - Not just respect for others' feelings and opinions, but for who they are.

Validate Others - Respect the emotions and needs of others. Emotions and needs are not debatable.

Lies, Tricks and Other Deceptions
How to Identify and Deal with Manipulators

Manipulative behaviors run the gamut of intensity from mere annoyance to criminal and civil harms, such as abuse, defamation and bribery.

Webster's New World Dictionary defines manipulation as "artful management, shrewd use of influence - especially in an unfair or fraudulent way - and falsification … for one's own purposes or profit." This definition assumes deliberate malice. I propose a broader definition.

People don't always think and act logically, and many manipulative behaviors involve no thought or planning. In other words, in personal relationships, manipulation is not necessarily a deliberate behavior. Still, unconscious manipulations can be as destructive as malicious manipulations; and everyone has the right of self-protection. As an alternative to the dictionary definition, please consider the following:

Manipulation is the use of inappropriate, unethical and indirect means for the purpose of meeting a personal need or desire.

One major problem is that we don't always know when we are being manipulated. This article identifies multiple manipulations to help you avoid being drawn into the manipulator's web of confusion and deceit.

Now, let's look at the manipulator's motives and methods. First, the manipulator fears being controlled. Thus, he strives to be in control of others. The second motive is to deny responsibility and accountability. The third motive stems from the manipulator's need to avoid consequences, such as humiliation, punishment and rejection.

Deep inside, the manipulator feels powerless and disconnected. She fears being open and direct, and attempts to satisfy her needs and wishes by being indirect and by tricking others. One surefire method is to exploit other people's emotions and to keep them off-balance.

In a relationship with a manipulator, equality is absent. The manipulator's view is that he is either 'one up' or 'one down.' If you have ever known some of the worst manipulators - narcissists and sociopaths, for example - you know that they have no interest in balanced and equal relationships.

When you suspect you are being manipulated, and you believe it's time to act, remember:

> ***Do not deal with a manipulator when your emotions are in charge of you.***
> ***A manipulator cannot harm you unless you allow it.***
> ***You cannot be manipulated if you don't want or need anything from the manipulator.***

Take another look at the Manipulation section in Part 2. Before engaging with a manipulator, take the time to put yourself in a balanced mind-body state. The skills in Part 1 can help you achieve that state.

Now, let's look at the many ways people try to mess with us.

Aggressions

It's All Your Fault!
Blaming others comes naturally. Every child has done it. At some point, however, you grow up and learn to accept responsibility … don't you?

The Switch
This is an especially aggressive form of blame. You've summoned up courage to confront an abuser. The abuser—or someone else in the picture —blames you for addressing/confronting him or her and makes you feel wrong, stupid, crazy or guilty.

You'd Better … Or Else!
This is an ultimatum, which is highly aggressive and can be considered bullying.

The Pre-emptive Strike
Your husband is cheating, and he suspects that you know about it. To put you on the defensive and to prevent you from accusing him, he goes on the offensive by accusing you of cheating.

The Button Pusher
Button pushing is a favorite of children and adolescents. It aims to get another person to lose control by provoking a strong emotion, especially anger. This includes name calling, challenging authority, threatening and blaming. When the person being provoked loses the ability to reason, (s)he loses the argument.

You'll Be Sorry!
Threatening self-harm is a form of manipulation that is not easy to deal with. It takes experience to distinguish a real threat from a manipulation, and the threat must not be underestimated. Input from others who've been through this ordeal or seeking professional guidance might be necessary.

Let's Make A Deal
The manipulator, a young girl, suggests to her parent how she should be punished in order to get a reduced 'sentence.' For example, she has done something wrong and doesn't want to be grounded. Rather than explaining why she doesn't deserve to be grounded, she offers to make a deal, such as promising to do x, y or z in the future if she's not grounded now.

You Owe Me!

Have you ever known someone who's done an awful lot for you, even without your requesting help? At some point, he wants payback. The manipulation is in using the unsolicited giving as a way to build up good will, which he'll collect later, maybe with interest.

Big Fat Bully

Whether you're horizontally challenged or not, threatening, hurting and intimidating others is just not nice.

What's Wrong With You? Everybody Does It!

Guys have used this and girls have heard this too many times. Sadly, some girls give in.

I'm Gonna Blow!

Kids love this one. A manipulator will threaten to explode or to run away in order to forestall a negative consequence.

A Sick Game

This manipulation seems direct, because it's an obvious power play. But is it really direct?

A wife gladly accepts her domineering husband's control and she blindly trusts his decisions.In effect she is telling him, 'I can't manage certain things – you take charge.' He wants to feel powerful because, deep inside, he feels weak. The manipulation appears straightforward. But in examining the situation closely, we see that both people are seeking to meet their needs without asserting them directly. The communication between them is unspoken and, thus, indirect.

It looks as if one is the 'loser' and the other is the 'winner.' But, in reality, each one is manipulating the other. The manipulator wins by looking and feeling superior. The subject wins by avoiding the risk taking responsibility and of being wrong. Even though both agree to it, this is inappropriate, because it damages the personal growth of both people. The manipulator, believing herself superior and deserving of royal treatment, ceases to grow, while the subject maintains his sense of incompetence. You see why I call this a sick game.

The Grinder

If you're a parent, you know this one. Your child wants something and will not let up, until you give in. They badger and hound you, until you can't take it any longer, and you relent.

Scare Tactics and Humiliation

You Can't Quit Me - You'll Never Find Anyone Else.

This manipulative tactic works with a partner who suffers from low self-esteem. The manipulator uses fear to enforce loyalty. The manipulator insinuates that the subject is undesirable and unable to take care of herself. He reminds her that she has no chance of controlling him or her situation.

'The Sky is Falling!' – The Fear-Monger

This manipulation is expressed as a demand for immediate action from others in order to address a fake emergency. The message is that there is no time to waste; hesitating would mean certain disaster. An everyday example is one that you have probably heard on television commercials. "This offer will not last. Supplies are running out. Call now!"

Baiting – A Variation Of The Button-Pusher

Baiting is the attempt to make someone say or do something that will humiliate him publicly. For example, a manipulator might tell someone a rumor about a hot topic, hoping that he will pass it on, and look stupid in the process. Or, trying to inflame someone's anger by provoking a reaction that will make her look foolish. By humiliating her, the manipulator feels superior.

Deliberate Deceptions

Crying Wolf

In the old fable, a young shepherd is "The Boy Who Cried Wolf". He takes pleasure in seeing the townspeople's confused scrambling, as they repeatedly run to his aid. The moral of the fable is, "No one believes a liar, even when he is telling the truth."

A powerful variation of this form of manipulation is a desperate plea for attention, which I call "crash and burn." The manipulator senses that no one is paying attention and is unable to assert his needs (remember, the manipulator is never direct or straightforward). So, he makes someone pay attention. His life becomes a soap opera, and he goes from crisis to crisis. Whenever he needs help, he says he's overwhelmed and can't cope. Eventually he burns out all his friends and is living with 25 cats.

Gossip

"Did you hear what Justin said about you?" "Guess who's pregnant." Not everyone would view this as a manipulation, but think again, please. This is a way of gaining attention and status by claiming to know the latest dirt. If you need to feel important, take the direct route. Do something that benefits others.

Stalling

This is another way that the avoidance pattern plays out. The manipulator avoids direct and honest confrontation by making the subject wait.

Trapping

A married couple are active church members. The marriage is in crisis. He wants a divorce, but cannot get it on religious grounds because neither has been unfaithful so he leaves false clues that he has cheated, and arranges for his wife to meet an attractive man. He hopes she will be angry and cheat for revenge. She takes the bait. He catches her and divorces her.

The False Promise
Russia and the United States agree on mutual nuclear disarmament. And both say, "You first."

I Changed My Mind
This is a variation of The False Promise. The difference here is that the False Promise is intended to deceive. Habitually changing your mind after giving your word, however, is not always deliberate. Still, it shows a lack of awareness of—even a hostility toward—another's welfare. It also may be an indirect expression of anger.

The Winning Smile
A smile can mean any number of things, such as a connection of friendship, a form of approval or a warm welcome. However, when the intent is to use another person, a smile becomes a weapon. Many people report being manipulated by a charmer who knows just how to use that sweet expression in order to mask a hidden motive. And they can't seem to say no to his lovable face, the twinkle in his eye. How can she bear to disappoint someone who has given her so much love and so much delight just by looking at her with that special look? What a charmer!

Shakespeare had it right when he wrote, "…meet it is that I set it down, That one may smile and smile and be a villain …" - Hamlet

Let's See If He Loves Me
Flirting to make one's spouse or partner jealous as a test of commitment is a direct form of manipulation.

Instant Intimacy
We all may know someone who shares too much personal information too soon. Awkward, isn't it? They seem to aim to fabricate a relationship with all its duties and obligations where no relationship yet exists. This is a way of getting a need met without putting the effort into forming a real relationship. Remember, the narcissistic manipulator has no desire for real relationships. This tactic works well when combined with guilt-tripping. When you come across Instant Intimacy, walk away and do not be drawn in.

The Mind Poisoner
Jealousy is spawned from the fear that some person will take away something or someone that is precious to us. Jealousy can drive people to devious behavior as they attempt to hold on to a loved one. Children are particularly at risk. It's not uncommon for a parent to use children as buffers within a tension-filled marriage and after a divorce. Imagine the custodial parent manipulating his child's beliefs and perceptions about his ex. And, the manipulation may be subtle. For instance, a parent might say, "I'd never say anything against my daughter's dad. A girl needs a father, and I won't say anything against him." Yet the bitterness of her non-verbal communications shows her true feelings.

Gaslighting

The term is taken from the title of the 1940's movie thriller Gaslight. The plot revolves around a man who connives to drive his wife insane by making her doubt her judgment and her perceptions.

When gaslighting, a manipulator aims to make the subject believe she is wrong, bad, stupid or crazy so that she becomes more dependent on him. The manipulator exploits that dependency for personal gain.

This trickery works in several ways. For example, the manipulator says one thing and later on denies it. He leaves the subject wondering if she is hearing things. He confuses her by using lots of words and talking fast. He can use a hostile approach, or, what's more dangerous, a mild manner. In the latter case he acknowledges her failings with a little laugh, as if to say, "that's all right, dear, I know you get things wrong from time to time. And I forgive you."

In either case, the subject's gut instinct (see "Trust Your Gut") may signal that something is not right. If she does not acknowledge what her gut tells her and ignores warning signs, she is an easy target.

Mystification

Mystification is a way to maintain power over others by claiming special power, knowledge or status. The manipulator uses obscure or professional language to demonstrate her superiority, implicitly underscoring the dependence of her subject. The use of mystification is meant to cement the top dog position, and it works well on uneducated, unstable and emotionally needy people. This is a standard ploy of cult leaders and criminal ringleaders.

Call me "Iago"

In Shakespeare's play Othello, Iago is the villain. Iago is an absolute master of malicious manipulation, using rumor in order to sow discord. Such a manipulator defames one or more people in order to gain personal advantage, for revenge to inflict harm, or for mere amusement. This goes far beyond mere gossip. When the rumors include planting seeds of doubt, suspicion and jealousy, as Iago does, the results can be devastating.

Never Give A Sucker An Even Break

A con artist justifies his exploitation of others by describing them as suckers. Manipulators believe their subjects are weak, ignorant, emotionally needy or greedy. To the manipulator, the subjects are fair game.

Laying Down For The Big Money

This tactic is an age-old pool hustler's trick. The manipulator pretends to be weak or incompetent in order to provoke his opponent to lower his guard. Then, when he raises the stakes—"Let's go double or nothing"—he wins. It works even better when the sucker suggests raising the stakes.

And better yet, when the manipulator just barely wins. Golfers, beware. This happens on the links, too.

They Went That-A-Way!
The official term for this manipulation is "disinformation." In a deliberate attempt, a manipulator provides bad information to avoid confrontation or to distract an adversary.

Minimizing
The feeling of shame naturally leads to minimizing one's misbehaviors. Most people want to avoid humiliation, but facing that emotional pain directly and seeking help is the constructive route. We might say this is a form of self-manipulation, or lying to oneself.

Crocodile Tears
This is a tearful and false admission of wrongdoing intended to earn leniency or to avoid punishment altogether.

Showers Of Kisses
Often used in combination with Crocodile Tears, a manipulator/abuser resorts to high levels of affections after the abuse becomes too intense for the subject to tolerate. He gives gifts and lots of attention. He begs for forgiveness, and pretends to be weak and stupid, saying things such as, "I don't know what gets into me." Or, "I'm such an idiot, how do you put up with me?" In this abuse pattern the subject falls for the apology, forgives him, and enables the abuse/manipulation cycle to restart.

I Was Just Trying To Help!
Using this excuse to gossip or to correct people is not acceptable.

"I Didn't Know."
Playing dumb is another form of lying.

The Flatterer
Flattery is not the same as honest praise. Flattery is meant to benefit the flatterer. Honest praise is given to encourage and reward good behavior. This is an important distinction in close relationships.

The Art Of One-Upmanship
One-upmanship is a term created several decades ago by the English humorist Stephen Potter. This tactic is an attempt to elevate one's status by taking the moral high ground against an adversary in order to gain an advantage by humiliating him or her. Imagine the manipulator is playing tennis with an acquaintance, and a young lady, whom both guys are interested in, is watching. The manipulator is losing. In order to score points with the lady, he offers his opponent the benefit of the doubt when, for example, a ball might have been in or out of bounds. Or he pretends to sprain an ankle and insists, "It's nothing, let's play on."

The Dependent

The behavior once termed passive-aggressive is now called dependent behavior. The purpose of such behavior is to evade responsibility and to avoid criticism and humiliation. Being wrong is unbearable for the dependent type; it's a slam on his entire being. Rather than claim personal responsibility, the Dependent refuses to make a decision and gets the other person to make the call, and, if there's a problem, take the fall.

For example, a groom planning a wedding with his fiancee is trying to decide where to hold the wedding reception. His fiancée doesn't care because his family is paying for the reception. But, being a guy, he doesn't know about banquet halls, so he tells her he can't decide. She suggests The Aquiline Meadows, and he says, "Nah, not enough parking." She offers the Midnight in Moscow night club, and he says, "Too ethnic." She suggests The Crystal Crutch, and he says, "Wrong side of town." She says, "Well, how about The Hilton?" He finally says, "Might as well." In effect, he's made the choice by negating her suggestions. And the beauty of it is, if it doesn't work out, he can blame her because, "Hey, I didn't pick the place!"

Appeals to Guilt and Plays for Sympathy

Mom The Martyr

How many martyr mothers does it take to change a light bulb? None! "It's alright, don't worry, I'll sit in the dark." This manipulator uses passive aggressive tactics and describes herself as long-suffering, undeserving or weak in order to gain sympathy or to avoid unwanted treatment. And, in fairness to moms, it doesn't have to be a mom, or even a female. Anyone can play the martyr.

Poor Me

This tactic is an indirect way of trying to meet a need for attention or sympathy. We probably all know someone who plays the perpetual victim, constantly vying for acknowledgement and support.

An extreme form of this manipulation is Munchausen Syndrome, a mental disorder in which someone constantly claims to be ill in order to get attention and even pity. A truly wicked extension of this disorder is Munchausen by Proxy, most often perpetrated by a mother upon her child and the medical establishment. The child is suffering from ongoing ailments, and gets frequent medical attention. The mother, in caring for her child, is sometimes using advanced medical knowledge and looks like a saint. In truth, the mother is actively and purposely harming or even poisoning her child in order to win sympathy and to underscore her suffering and heroism.

If You Really Love Me

If someone doubts his spouse's or partner's devotion, the proper way to communicate one's displeasure is to use the 'I' statement, described in Part 1.

However, manipulators are not comfortable being honest and direct. Rather than being up front, they challenge and guilt-trip. For example, "If you really love me, you won't go to that party, you'll stay home, you'll stop talking to that guy." Etc., etc., etc.

The Fisherman
Fishing for compliments is no crime. But habitually demeaning yourself so that others will build you up is an indirect ploy for attention and praise.

I'm So Confused
Confusion is something that happens to you, rather than something you choose. Right? Well, try this idea on for size. If you're constantly befuddled, is the confusion truly a reaction to outside influences? Or, could your perpetual daze be an automatic, learned strategy aimed at having others rush to your aid? Does staying confused help you evade responsibilities? What if it's meant to protect you from the consequences of a bad decision? Doesn't look so innocent now, does it? Looks kind of like the Dependent.

Triangulating
Seeking an ally, the manipulator draws a third person into a two-person conflict. The third party's proper response should be, "I ain't got a dog in this here fight!"

When Momma Says, "No" and Daddy Says, "Yes"
Using this tactic, a manipulator pits one person against another in order to get what he wants.

Distractions

Bubble Gum Girl
Using this tactic, a manipulator gets someone else to do her dirty work. For example, "the Bubble Gum Girl" asks her friend Ashley to ask Justin if her likes her. This is an anxiety-ridden attempt to avoid rejection, and it's not Ashley's job. However, if Ashley heartily agrees, there's no problem. On the other hand, Ashley may feel obligated to help her friend out, and may not feel good about it. This confusion of personal responsibility can happen for adults, as well as kids. Some of you may have seen it in your own families, or in the workplace.

Push-Pull
The manipulator keeps others off balance or at arm's length by regularly shifting his degree of closeness to them. The manipulator fears closeness because any attachment to another person opens him up to being controlled and potentially hurt by that person. However, at some point in a relationship, intimacy demands that we make ourselves vulnerable and transparent. If the manipulator feels especially ashamed or inferior, he can't bear to be seen as he really is. He'll sabotage the relationship rather than risk exposure.

Hey, Look Over There!

Using this tactic, a manipulator removes attention from core issues by raising an irrelevant side issue or a "red herring." This is another example of avoidance.

Making Light

The manipulator habitually uses jokes when conversations get serious. When the other person is unhappy and needs to talk seriously, this behavior is unacceptable.

Titillation

The Last Minute Bomb

Therapists know all about this. Some of us call it "the doorknob confession." At the end of a session a client—perhaps with her hand on the doorknob, preparing to exit—says something like, "Oh, by the way, I should probably tell you ... uh ... you know that man I've been having an affair with? Well, I'm pregnant. You won't tell my husband, right?" Exit, stage left.

The Silent Treatment

This is an extremely powerful manipulation. The manipulator is angry, resentful and wants payback. The other person wants to talk, but he wants her to stew in her own juice. What's she to do? Absolutely, positively be open and direct about how this affects her. See the 'I' Statement in Part 1, and review the "I" Statement reloaded at the start of Part 3.

The Combo Platter

Have you known someone who's especially good at bending your mind? By the time he's done talking, you don't know what to believe. Effective manipulators don't depend on one method alone. As you become skilled in observing various manipulations, you'll begin to notice that the really clever manipulators know how to combine them for maximum impact. And, there are some devious combinations out there. Keep your eyes and ears open. This could be a fascinating study and a surprising education for you.

A special note for parents: it's not always easy to tell whether your child is manipulating, or if he's simply testing the waters - and, as you probably know, testing limits a normal part of a child's development. If the child continues pushing limits, even after the rules and boundaries have been clearly spelled out, that's a manipulation.

If your happiness is being affected by a manipulator, what can you do? First, ask yourself whether this situation can change. If not, that's the end of the discussion, and in that case you have a bigger problem. If you believe change is possible, ask yourself if you are ready to make that change. At that point you can proceed as follows.

Ask yourself the following questions. What am I afraid of? What do want or need from the manipulator? What am I doing that allows the manipulator to succeed? How much influence do I have in this situation? What must I give up in order to be free of the manipulator's power? Will it be worth it? What can I look forward to once I am free of the manipulation?

It can also be helpful to consult someone for a reality check—someone you trust who relates to you without judging or advising. Leave no stone unturned in the search for knowledge and wisdom. Professional therapy, books, Internet articles, blogs and support groups are excellent resources. The information is out there.

The Rules of Engagement Questionnaire

This questionnaire helps you see your conflict resolution errors. By correcting just one of these, you'll notice a big difference and feel much better. If you can address all of them, you'll become a conflict resolution superstar! Please, be encouraged; everyone makes some of these errors.

After you and your spouse or partner read each other's circled answers, choose one error on the other person's list, and ask him or her to begin correcting it. After each of you has corrected one error, you can move on to correcting the others, one at a time. The skills in Part 1 will help.

If you are working with a counselor, you may do this exercise and get the counselor's feedback.

Circle your answers below each statement.

I jump right into resolving conflict without thinking about my mood.
| *never* | *rarely* | *sometimes* | *often* | *always* |

I keep going even after I or the other person has shown anger. I don't know how to cool down and start again.
| *never* | *rarely* | *sometimes* | *often* | *always* |

I start with a negative or sarcastic comment.
| *never* | *rarely* | *sometimes* | *often* | *always* |

I lecture or preach. I tell people what they need to do.
| *never* | *rarely* | *sometimes* | *often* | *always* |

I choose the wrong time and place.
| *never* | *rarely* | *sometimes* | *often* | *always* |

I "multitask" while resolving conflict.
| *never* | *rarely* | *sometimes* | *often* | *always* |

I bring in other people who have nothing to do with the conflict.
| *never* | *rarely* | *sometimes* | *often* | *always* |

I draw comparisons to others.
| *never* | *rarely* | *sometimes* | *often* | *always* |

I assume that I understand what the other person did, said or meant. I jump to conclusions.
| *never* | *rarely* | *sometimes* | *often* | *always* |

I try to define the motives of the other person. For example, I might say, "You're just trying to
_____." Or, "All you care about is _____."

       never   *rarely*   *sometimes*   *often*   *always*

I prepare my answer before the other person has finished talking. In that way, I stop listening.

       never   *rarely*   *sometimes*   *often*   *always*

I say "should" or "shouldn't," as in "You shouldn't feel that way." or "You should 'want' to do this because you love me!"

       never   *rarely*   *sometimes*   *often*   *always*

I talk more about the other person than I do about myself.

       never   *rarely*   *sometimes*   *often*   *always*

I blame or label others. I deny responsibility. Blaming often shows up in statements like, "You are so _____." "You're an _____."
"You never _____." or "You always _____."

       never   *rarely*   *sometimes*   *often*   *always*

I threaten, insult, put others down or make demands. I manipulate. Some manipulations include "bullying" (yelling, foul language, name-calling), "the silent treatment," "guilt-tripping," "crying wolf," and "gossiping."

       never   *rarely*   *sometimes*   *often*   *always*

I don't tell the full truth. I hold things back, which is a form of lying.

       never   *rarely*   *sometimes*   *often*   *always*

I lie about what I'm feeling. For example, I deny my negative feelings.

       never   *rarely*   *sometimes*   *often*   *always*

If I admit that I have negative feelings, I put myself down for having them.

       never   *rarely*   *sometimes*   *often*   *always*

I do not speak in neutral tones. I do a lot of negative body language—eye-rolling, snorting, sarcastic tone of voice, loud voice, mocking language.

       never   *rarely*   *sometimes*   *often*   *always*

I vent anger in the wrong way.

       never   *rarely*   *sometimes*   *often*   *always*

I don't stay on topic.

       never   *rarely*   *sometimes*   *often*   *always*

I dig up the past and use it as a weapon.

    never   *rarely*   *sometimes*   *often*   *always*

I walk out before the conflict is resolved.

    never   *rarely*   *sometimes*   *often*   *always*

I take things personally.

    never   *rarely*   *sometimes*   *often*   *always*

I am defensive.

    never   *rarely*   *sometimes*   *often*   *always*

I shut down when the conflict becomes too intense.

    never   *rarely*   *sometimes*   *often*   *always*

I am not sensitive to the needs, feelings and rights of the other person

    never   *rarely*   *sometimes*   *often*   *always*

I am critical and negative about the other person in general.

    never   *rarely*   *sometimes*   *often*   *always*

The Worldview Survey

Are you planning to enter into a committed relationship? If so, this survey can be a blessing to both of you. Knowing these things about each other can help prevent future disagreements, unpleasant surprises and conflicts. At the very least, it will spark a lively conversation and help you get to know each other on a deeper level.

Check the answer(s) closest to your belief, or add your own answer as "Other." It's generally best practice to do the survey separately, and then share your answers with your special person.

The World is
__Good
__Evil
__Neutral
__Dangerous
__Safe
__Challenging
__Fascinating
__Confusing
__Crazy
__Wonderful

Other _____

Life is
__A struggle
__An adventure
__A battle
__Joyful
__A test
__A journey
__A game
__A race
__Fun
__A gamble
__A pain in the rear
__Short
__Too long

Other _____

People are

__Basically good

__Basically bad

__Unreliable

__Fascinating

__Safe

__Selfish

__Dangerous

__Unpredictable

__Stupid

Other _____

Love is

__Wonderful

__Terrible

__Scary

__A game

__A myth

__Unattainable

__Confusing

__Hard work

__Too much trouble

__Worth the trouble

__A lie

Other _____

Courage is

__Feeling the fear and doing it anyway

__Not caring what others think of me at all, ever

__Showing others how strong you are

__Doing what you must, just because you must

__Being the first to try the next new thing

__Risking your welfare for a higher good

__Standing up for what you believe

Other _____

After death …

__There is nothing—there is no afterlife and no soul

__There is heaven or hell—your soul goes to one or the other

    Choose one:

        It depends on your actions and deeds

        It depends on the religion you choose

        It depends on your feelings

        It depends on your belief and faith

        It's God's decision and we have no control over that

        It's fate and we have no control over that

__Everyone goes to heaven

__Everyone goes to hell

__Reincarnation

__You meld with the cosmic spirit in eternal oneness

Other _____

My life motto is

__You get what you pay for.

__What goes around comes around.

__Life stinks, and then you die.

__I can have it all.

__You can't take it with you.

__Life is beautiful.

__The Golden Rule.

__Do unto others before they do unto you.

__Whoever dies with the most toys wins.

__Might makes right.

__Play it safe.

__Go along to get along.

__There's a sucker born every minute.

__Live life to the fullest.

__You can achieve anything you put your mind to.

__It's better to give than to receive.

__Dance as if there's no one watching.

Other _____

I trust

__Nobody
__Everybody
__My family and no one else
__My peers
__Easily
__God
__With difficulty
Other _____

Difficult people

__Are an unwelcome challenge
__Make me retreat
__Merit my sympathy
__Frustrate me
__Need help, and I'll try
__Need help, but not from me
__Make me laugh
__Should just get over themselves
__Make me agitated
__Get what they deserve
__Make me angry
__Need to be set straight
__Make me sad

Other _____

The purpose of life is

__To work hard and succeed
__To have just enough and no more
__To help and serve others
__To glorify God
__To find my mission or calling and fulfill it
__To avoid pain
__To seek pleasure and fun
__To be in complete control as much as possible
__To give and receive love
__To make a difference

Other _____

I'm afraid of

__Dying

__Being alone

__Conflict and stress

__The opposite sex

__Losing control

__Being close to someone

__Being abandoned

__Physical pain

__Not noticing something that might hurt me

__People

__Anything to do with religion

__Anything new or strange

Other _____

When it comes to money

__It's very important

__It's not important

__It's not my strong point

__It's something I know a lot about

__I'm a saver

__I'm a spender

__I am an impulsive shopper

__It's how I keep score

__I'm cautious

Other _____

When it comes to my future, I

__Have hope

__Feel worried and / or scared

__Don't care

__Just go with the flow

__Can't manage without a plan

__Don't want to think about it

__Need help

Other _____

Recreation and Play
__Should be part of everyone's life
__Is something I really enjoy
__Makes me apprehensive being with others
__Is a waste of time
__Makes me think of old people and retirement
__Means all-out playtime and fun, and nothing else
__Should involve some kind of competition

Other _____

When it seems I must change something (about myself or about anything else)
__I tend to resist
__I don't like it, but I'll do what I must
__It's a stimulating challenge
__I like routine and structure
__I feel overwhelmed and don't know where to start
__I ignore it
__I put it off
__I panic

Other _____

Happiness
__Is everyone's right
__Means feeling good about myself
__Is hard to grasp
__Is about feeling good about yourself
__Happiness? What's that?
__Is fleeting
__Is an illusion
__Means nothing to me
__Is a natural outgrowth of virtuous living
__Is about experiencing pleasure and enjoyment
__Is overrated—it's better to just be satisfied with your life

Other _____

Work

__Is a necessary evil
__Is a chance to express myself and my talents
__Is stressful—there's not much good about it
__Is about making money
__Gives me a sense of worth and value
__Is a duty
__Is a way to make my mark in the world
__Should be as short-lived as possible

Other _____

My opinion about sex is

__I love it
__It's overrated
__It's the most important part of a relationship
__Is dirty
__It's something I am not comfortable with
__It should be fun
__Is an expression of love
__Should only be for having children
__I need it to help me relax
__It's a royal pain
    Other _____

One thing I can count on is

__Even the best people will disappoint me
__I'll never have enough money
__I'll always be able to manage somehow
__My judgment and values
__Nothing
__Myself
__God
__My family
__There will always be something to worry about
__Things will work out, somehow

Other _____

About my life, I believe

__It's all been pre-determined and I have no control—it's fate

__My actions and attitude determine how my life comes out—it's my responsibility

__Other people are largely to blame for how my life has turned out

__Other people have nothing to do with how my life has turned out

__I can do anything I put my mind to

__I have blown a lot of chances and I just have to settle for whatever good I can get

__I mess up everything I try

__Even though I've not succeeded perfectly, I think I can make things work out

Other _____

When I feel uncertain or 'stuck,' I am motivated to make a decision by

__The promise of an immediate reward, no matter how small or big

__The promise of a better reward in the near or distant future

__The fear of a punishment or some other bad outcome

__The concern that staying stuck might hurt me in the long run

__The concern that staying stuck might hurt someone else

__I can't think of anything that would motivate me

Other _____

Honesty is

__Saying whatever comes to mind just as it's happening

__Telling the whole truth

__Letting others know your true self

__Never telling any kind of lie

__Always dealing fairly in business

__Being yourself

Other _____

Freedom is

__Permission to do anything you like

__Ability to go anywhere, anytime

__Being allowed to say anything you feel like saying

__Liberty in religious belief

__Not being responsible to anyone

__Never having to be poor

__Never feeling the fear of oppression

Other _____

The marital relationship is

___A partnership

___A trap

___A prison

___Enslavement of women

___A team of two people supporting each other

___A practical arrangement for mutual benefit

___A life mission together

___A wonderful romance

___Hard work

___Something that's expected of you

___For having children

___For continuing the family line

___The most important commitment one can make

___Is for life

___Monogamous only

___Open to all and any variations

Other _____

Children

___Are a great blessing from God

___Are fun to be with

___Deserve and need protection

___Start to learn about life before they can speak

___Are to be seen and not heard

___Should be the center of a marriage

___Must be taught to obey authority without questioning

___Have the right to be heard

___Should work for their allowance

___Must contribute to the family in some way, when they are able

___Must never contradict their parents

___Can save a bad relationship

___Are an essential part of a marriage

Other _____

I hate _____

_____

I love _____

_____

What makes me angry is _____

_____

What delights me is _____

_____

What saddens me is _____

_____

What's most important to me now is _____

_____

Final Thoughts

"... do not forget, and do not turn away from the words of my mouth. Get wisdom; get insight. Do not forsake her, and she will keep you; love her, and she will guard you. The beginning of wisdom is this: Get wisdom, and whatever you get, get insight." - Proverbs 4: 5-7

Daily practice will help you be consistent in applying what you have learned here. Even so, nearly all of us know someone who lost weight or quit smoking … but later on, they experienced the dreaded backslide. That might happen to you from time to time, but if you are careful, it won't be an ongoing problem.

Incidentally, top athletes know how to forestall a backslide. They do not take success for granted, and they prevent backsliding by practicing fundamentals every day. No matter how many medals or championships they've won, they continue to work with their coaches. For them, success is not about awards; it's about continual improvement. They focus on eliminating weaknesses and building on strengths. They train their minds and bodies to be highly self-aware.

Keep on learning about yourself. Gather information about relationships and behavior. Read, listen to audio recordings, hang out with smart, successful, positive-minded people. Be part of a group of supportive folks who also want to grow in wisdom and maturity. Use every available tool and information source. Books, the Internet, workshops, classes, etc.

However, be careful. Do not believe everything you hear, see or read. Just as great wisdom is available, false teaching and bad information are just as available. Learn to think critically. When you encounter any statement that claims to be true, test it. Demand to know the evidence. If you're not sure what critical thinking is, find out! The information is there. All you need to do is to look for it.

It is hoped that you now see the importance of wisdom, as well as skills and knowledge in the handling of conflict. Be curious. Never stop learning. As you continue to handle conflict with wisdom and kindness, you will make a difference. You will inspire others to spread the message that what really matters in life is love. And it is through our relationships that our living expression of love will leave a beauty mark on this world.

About the Author

Robert Kallus is a licensed psychotherapist, practicing in Valparaiso, Indiana. He is an active member of The American Society of Clinical Hypnosis, America's oldest organization for licensed professionals who practice hypnosis, The Chicago Society of Clinical Hypnosis, and is a Diplomate of The American Institute of Stress. He employs evidence-based approaches, including Cognitive Behavioral Therapy, hypnotherapy, and cranial electrotherapy stimulation. In addition, trauma treatments include Eye Movement Desensitization and Reprocessing Therapy (EMDR) and Trauma-Focused Cognitive Behavioral Therapy. The author has practiced transcendental meditation since 1971, and teaches mindfulness meditation to many of his clients.

In 2004, the author and his colleagues at a residential treatment center for teens created workshops on communication, conflict resolution, anger management and stress management for families and their children. As the director of this program and as Program Director of the facility, he expanded the scope of these workshops, wrote the workshop manuals, hired and trained a team of workshop presenters, and taught thousands of people in hundreds of workshops at the treatment center and at churches and camps.

Further information about the author is available at: www.robertkallustherapy.com.

Made in the USA
Monee, IL
06 November 2021